WEED

Para la Ciudad de México, la capital del hemisferio,
por ser mi hogar y maestra

Zest Books™
An imprint of Lerner Publishing Group, Inc.
241 First Avenue North
Minneapolis, MN 55401 USA

For reading levels and more information, look up this title at www.lernerbooks.com.
Visit us at zestbooks.net. 🖪 🖾

Designed by Athena Currier.
Main body text set in Univers LT Std and Janson Text LT Std.
Typefaces provided by Adobe Systems.

Library of Congress Cataloging-in-Publication Data

Names: Donohue, Caitlin, author.
Title: Weed : cannabis culture in the Americas / Caitlin Donohue.
Description: Minneapolis : Zest Books, [2023] | Includes bibliographical references and index. | Audience: Ages 14–18 | Audience: Grades 10–12 | Summary: "Culture writer Caitlin Donohue uses interviews with medical researchers, educators, activists, artists, business leaders, and other experts to craft an inclusive and comprehensive overview of cannabis in the Western Hemisphere for young adults" —Provided by publisher.
Identifiers: LCCN 2022052448 (print) | LCCN 2022052449 (ebook) | ISBN 9781728429533 (library binding) | ISBN 9781728429540 (paperback) | ISBN 9798765602416 (ebook)
Subjects: LCSH: Cannabis—America—Juvenile literature.
Classification: LCC HV5822.C3 D666 2023 (print) | LCC HV5822.C3 (ebook) | DDC 362.29/5—dc23/eng/20230221

LC record available at https://lccn.loc.gov/2022052448
LC ebook record available at https://lccn.loc.gov/2022052449

Manufactured in the United States of America
1-49454-49519-3/6/2023

WEED

CANNABIS CULTURE
in the AMERICAS

CAITLIN DONOHUE

Z ZEST BOOKS
MINNEAPOLIS

CONTENTS

Part 3: The Fight for Drug War Justice

INTRODUCTION

When I was fifteen, I consumed cannabis for the first time. My friend and I walked to a nearby elementary school, not too late at night, and smoked mid(dle-grade weed) from a pipe. There were fine boys involved, though apologies to them, because I don't remember anything else about our male companionship that evening, or even how the weed hit, much less where it came from. I didn't get high the first time I smoked, but I did the second. Marijuana was OK, I decided, but I was busy with high school classes and extracurriculars, couldn't consume in my house for perhaps obvious reasons (my parents were cool, but not *that* cool), and getting stoned seemed to involve free time that, frankly, a student-athlete doesn't have.

College was another story. I hated the small private school I went to, which was really far from where I'd grown up. I had good teachers and liked my coursework, but I didn't relate to the people around me. Long story short, I got pretty depressed. To deal, I would get stupid high passing joints around with my boyfriend, who sold cannabis. Or even cuter: I'd hit a gravity bong in someone's dorm room when I was drunk and end up puking. Luckily, I mellowed out on marijuana in my twenties. Nowadays, cannabis and I have a lovely, balanced relationship that assists my creativity, calms my anxiety, and helps me enjoy trashy TV series.

This is great, because as an even younger pup, drugs scared me to death. In middle school, I remember the anxiety—no doubt caused by mainstream media's messaging—that swept over me on my daily walk home. I would inevitably pass a group of older kids who smoked on the sidewalk after class (probably cigarettes, but in my *Reefer Madness*–addled mind, they could have been using *marijuana*!). I know now that in my fear, I was unfairly stigmatizing people for consuming psychoactive substances—and freaking myself out for no real reason.

How'd I eventually arrive at a more measured attitude toward psychoactive substances? First, my tension had to peak, thanks to good old, crime 'n' punishment–based traditional drug education. One day in sixth grade, our class received a Just Say No lesson, which, if I recall correctly, revolved around our imminent moral and physical downfall should we ever ingest an illegal substance.

When my mom got home from work that day, I cornered her. "*Mom*, did you know that there are things called drugs, and that the people who do them are *bad*?"

Again, my parents are cool. "People who do drugs aren't bad," my mom replied. "In fact, your mom has done drugs." Her words undid me—for a moment, I considered my own safety with this deviant, drug-doing mother. But as time went on, the memory of what she said calmed my fearful reaction to cannabis consumption. The modern-day march toward greater acceptance of marijuana has also helped. I'm not going to say that, even today, I have a role-model relationship with psychoactive substances. There have been moments in which I've used too many drugs or ingested them during inopportune situations. (Hell, to this day I can't give up drinking coffee despite the stomachaches I get. Convince me that caffeine is not a hard drug!)

I am sharing my personal marijuana voyage with you because I think people should talk more about drugs, as they should talk more about any complex topic that impacts our lives. How are we supposed to be safe when it comes to cannabis if we're terrified of admitting that we're curious about it, or that someone we care about has been getting high? What's more, by treating the drug as a taboo subject, we could miss out on learning the full history of our own communities.

Humankind has used *Cannabis sativa* for some twelve thousand years, originally as a source of fiber and nutrition during the early Neolithic era in East Asia. People have used the drug as a way to get high for about twenty-five hundred years. The earliest records of medicinal uses of the plant come from China, where it is called ma and was used to treat a variety of health conditions.

Terms You Need to Know

This stuff can get confusing.

- *Cannabis sativa*: the scientific name for a leafy, flowering plant that originated in East Asia and whose diverse varietals are grown around the world for industrial, recreational, medicinal, spiritual, and culinary uses
- **Marijuana:** *Cannabis sativa* that is rich in THC or consumed for recreational purposes
- **Hemp:** *Cannabis sativa* that is grown for its strong fibers as well as its therapeutic, medicinal, and other properties. There is no scientific difference between hemp and marijuana, though many governments have put the cutoff between the two around 0.01 to 0.03 percent THC to regulate the plant.
- **Cannabinoid:** certain chemical compounds found in cannabis
- **Tetrahydrocannabinol (THC):** the cannabinoid most famous for getting people high when it is consumed; also an important medicinal tool

Ancient Hindus, Assyrians, Greeks, and Romans also used the plant as medicine. Africa was another early hub of cannabis culture, where people used pipes to ingest the drug as far back as the 1300s. Many scholars believe that Africans introduced the American continents to psychoactive uses of weed when enslaved people managed to bring seeds on their forced journey across the Atlantic. In the mid-nineteenth century, an Irish doctor brought knowledge of medicinal weed back to the UK from India. Because of his work, Europeans and white Americans began taking cannabis for stomach pain and other health conditions.

The drug's ensuing widespread use among white people persisted roughly until 1937. That's when the United States banned

- **Cannabidiol (CBD):** a cannabinoid that is especially prized for its anti-inflammatory and other medicinal and therapeutic properties. It is the main ingredient of many widely used cannabis-based pharmaceutical drugs, including Epidiolex, the first such medicine approved by the United States' Food and Drug Administration.
- **Psychoactive:** drugs that affect the brain and often cause changes in mood and behavior
- **Medicinal:** substances with healing properties
- **Prohibition:** to ban something
- **War on Drugs:** also called the Drug War, a failed worldwide government initiative in the twentieth and twenty-first centuries that seeks to end the consumption of illegal psychoactive substances. Its policies usually increased targeting and strict punishments of people who use or sell illegal drugs or both.

cannabis in a fit of anti-Mexican and anti-Black xenophobic (based on the fear of people born in other countries) and racist panic driven by the country's first drug czar, Harry Anslinger. The United States was not the first country to make cannabis illegal, but it proved to be the most influential in spreading prohibitionist policies around the world. The subsequent, nearly worldwide ban on cannabis limited our knowledge of the plant's many medicinal properties, and the uneven way in which cannabis bans are enforced has contributed to global inequality. Today, studies suggest that people of different races use and sell cannabis at roughly equal rates but that people from many communities of color are arrested and incarcerated for cannabis-related crimes at much higher rates. In light of this injustice, we should be aware that drugs impact people's lives in ways that go far beyond personal consumption.

Fortunately, researchers continue to expand our knowledge of *Cannabis sativa*, partly due to a growing recognition of the drug's medicinal properties. In 1988 Saint Louis University School of Medicine researchers discovered that THC, one of the psychoactive compounds found in cannabis, can activate brain receptors in rodents. Further investigation showed that human bodies—and likely the bodies of many animals—include a biological network known as the endocannabinoid system, which responds to cannabis. Global governments are expanding research on the drug, and recent findings point toward weed's positive impact on symptoms of post-traumatic stress disorder (PTSD), glaucoma, and in helping to end opioid dependency. As of 2023, nearly fifty countries have legalized some form of medicinal marijuana. Uruguay, Canada, South Africa, and thirty-seven US states (and Washington, DC) have legalized recreational cannabis. Global cannabis sales are predicted to top $61 billion by 2026. Despite these numbers, having or selling cannabis is still punished with jail time and even death in many of the countries that prohibit weed.

What's in a *Weed*?

People use a variety of words to refer to cannabis. *Marijuana* and *weed*, of course, but also historic or place-specific terms such as *reefer, maconha, ganja, pot, the devil's lettuce, bud, mota,* and on and on. In the legalization era, some advocates have called for the drug to be referred to only as *cannabis*. That's because most of these other words come from the prohibition era. For example, the US media and government started calling it *marijuana* as part of the anti-Mexican racist propaganda that led to it becoming illegal. But the importance of acknowledging these histories of oppression—especially what they mean for the continuing Drug War—is why I'm an advocate for using all the words for weed that we've got. I go back and forth between referring to marijuana as a drug and a plant because it is both.

Hemp, which refers to varietals of *Cannabis sativa*, is used in a wide range of products, including paper, rope, and animal feed. This field of industrial hemp is growing in Queenstown, Maryland.

This book is an attempt to make sense of these contradictions and the wildly different roles that cannabis plays in the Western Hemisphere. It is made up of seventeen interviews with cannabis experts from Canada, Argentina, and many countries in between. Some live where the drug is almost entirely illegal, while others live where it's considered a gourmet item or essential medicine. Some interviewees are politicians; some are activists. Others are fashion designers or magazine editors. So varied are their experiences that sometimes it's difficult to believe they're all talking about the same plant! We did many of the interviews in Spanish, and I translated their answers afterward. When you see words or phrases in brackets [like so], that's me explaining something that was left out of the conversation or adding background information.

But who am I to take you on this journey through the world of weed? Originally from the United States, I first started writing

Cannabis was used to treat various medical conditions long before its prohibition. Countries are slowly lifting restrictions on the plant, particularly for medicinal purposes.

Weed

about cannabis a decade ago in a San Francisco newspaper column. I have spent the last eight years as a Mexico City–based journalist, and I host a radio show about drug culture and politics. My adoptive country is an extremely important place for cannabis. Mexico is likely where the word "marijuana" was coined, and for decades, it grew the weed that was smoked by much of the world—certainly, stoners in the United States relied on Mexico for their supply. Living here has educated me on how the rest of the world perceives certain things about the United States—things that many of us who grew up there don't learn. High on this list is the way in which the United States spreads its influence around the globe by military invasion, covert intelligence operations, or even economic penetration by private companies—an extremely complex process often called US imperialism.

Here's another thing I've learned: Mexico has been deeply and tragically impacted by the War on Drugs. It has become the site of a showdown between the country's corrupt government and powerful narcos (narcotraficantes, or people who move large quantities of drugs as part of an organized crime group, called a cartel). Between 2006 and 2018, 125,000 to 150,000 Mexican lives were lost to Drug War–related murders, according to a 2020 US Congress report. This hyper-violent conflict surges on, partly because of the cartels' sale of illegal drugs, mostly bought by US users. Many Mexican cannabis advocates push for the legalization of weed to give consumers, both nationally and in the US, the option to buy from non-cartel suppliers, and in so doing, help defund the Drug War.

Seeing how the cannabis economy works on both sides of the US-Mexico border has been a unique education. It has helped me to understand the War on Drugs and cannabis legalization as international issues.

The point of this book is not to encourage you to consume cannabis! But you may already have tried it—and that's fine too.

Prohibition Has Always Been Racist

The racist dimensions of cannabis policing are part of the history of prohibition being used by governments and other authorities to oppress communities of color. Some of the first antidrug laws (besides ordinances against alcohol) in the Americas were the Catholic Church's 1620 prohibition of peyote, a hallucinogenic cactus used in Indigenous spiritual rites, and San Francisco's 1875 ban on establishments that served opium, a drug that had traditionally been used by many Chinese residents.

Thirty-nine percent of US twelfth graders in a 2021 study said they had smoked marijuana at least once, and many others consume medicinal cannabis. *If* you want my opinion, I'd say hold off on using it regularly without a doctor's recommendation at least until you're well out of your teens, given that scientific data on the effects of cannabis on young brains is still inconclusive. I imagine you don't need to be reminded of this, but very real legal and social repercussions exist for many youth who consume or possess the drug.

Whatever choice you make, having candid discussions about marijuana falls under harm reduction—that we should be trying to minimize the negative effects of psychoactive substances on their users rather than trying to end their use. People have consumed drugs—and often with positive effects—since nearly the dawn of our species, and attempting to end that relationship is illogical as well as completely unrealistic. We need to talk about weed to keep ourselves and those around us safe.

You're going to come away from these interviews knowing more about cannabis than most adults in your life. Try to be humble about it . . . or not. You'll probably also wind up with more questions than when you started reading, because we are dealing with some complex subjects here. This book is only a jumping-off point in your cannabis education. One reason is because as a society, we still don't know a lot about marijuana. For a long time, the restrictions on cannabis made it very hard to get legal permission to conduct scientific investigations on the drug's effects. Continuing stigma makes a lot of people with cannabis experience hesitant to talk publicly, and a lot of data that has to do with marijuana and public policy is nonexistent. Hell, it's still nearly impossible to calculate how many people are imprisoned for cannabis-related crimes in the United States (some estimates put the figure at forty thousand, as of 2022. The cannabis pardons that were announced by President Joe Biden in October of that year may reduce that number, though it is unclear how many individuals they will wind up impacting.) As marijuana access widens, these restrictions on information will probably become less severe. Watch for new sources of information that are in depth, up to date, include acknowledgment of any political bias they may have, and are produced by people who have demonstrated knowledge in the field.

I would love it if you reported back about what you're learning. As you may have noticed, I'm always down to talk about weed.

—Caitlin Donohue, Mexico City, May 5, 2022

Part 1

CANNABIS AND OUR BODIES

CHAPTER 1

A Drug We Have to Talk About

Emily Jenkins, Registered Nurse and Associate Professor

What have you learned in school about drugs and the people who consume them? Have your teachers taught you about why people do drugs or how to have a healthy relationship with psychoactive substances? If you're reading this book, you probably know that something's not quite right about the way most educational systems cover cannabis. Abstinence-based curriculums—whose lessons are focused on the frightening consequences of casual drug use—can come across as more of a threat than an opportunity to learn.

Many of the most popular antidrug educational programs were inspired by Just Say No, a motto popularized in the 1980s by Nancy Reagan, then the US First Lady. She sought to present drug use as the moral failure of individuals without addressing its social context. The prohibition-minded Drug Abuse Resistance Education (D.A.R.E.) program takes Just Say No as its jumping-off point, and it is still popular in US schools. The program was created in the early '80s by LA police chief Daryl Gates, who was later forced to resign because of accusations of racism among his officers and the Los Angeles Unified School District. But police officers continued to deliver D.A.R.E. lectures in schools, relaying firsthand accounts of locking up drug consumers and workers. Despite its popularity, D.A.R.E. has been found to have zero long-term effect on keeping kids away from drugs.

Just Say No–inspired policies often lead schools to criminalize students who use cannabis by suspending or expelling them—or even referring them to law enforcement. These policies are driven by the same racism and other biases that studies find in the policing of adult cannabis use. Statistics show that Black, Latino, disabled, and LGBTQIA+ students all experience school punishment at elevated rates.

First Lady Nancy Reagan (*center*) traveled across the United States using her influence and position to support the antidrug campaign "Just Say No," even hosting a rally at the White House on May 22, 1986. School-sponsored antidrug programs focused on abstinence were prevalent throughout the 1980s and 1990s, and some variations of these programs continue to be utilized in schools throughout the country.

Smart people such as Emily Jenkins are working on new forms of youth drug education. An associate professor at Canada's University of British Columbia's School of Nursing, Jenkins lives in the second country in the world to legalize recreational marijuana. (Canada is also the headquarters of many of the planet's largest transnational cannabis corporations.) To understand how best to educate young people about drugs in a rapidly shifting legal landscape, Jenkins oversees scientific studies based on interviews with teens about their relationship with cannabis and other psychoactive substances. She believes that young people know best about what kinds of educational messages will keep them safe, educated, and healthy.

Emily Jenkins and her team have been interviewing young people about cannabis for over a decade. Based on these conversations, they have created educational resources about the plant's use that feature stories of people's lived experiences using the plant.

The registered nurse sat down with me for a frank discussion on what science does and does not know about the impacts cannabis has on teens' bodies and lives. Most important, she advised on figuring out whether you've tipped into problematic usage of any drug, and what to do if you have.

EMILY JENKINS

Very Little *Conclusive* Scientific Evidence

The question about the physical effects of cannabis on the body has been one of great interest, especially in recent decades. One of the challenges in answering it is that cannabis has been illegal in much of North America for the last one hundredish years. This has limited the types of research that can be done about the effects it has on teen bodies. While there's lots of information out there about risks and benefits of cannabis use, there's actually very little *conclusive* scientific evidence to support these claims. That's been a significant barrier in terms of understanding long-term patterns of use, developing therapeutic models, and also understanding the physical effects. A helpful resource in recent years is a 2017 report from the National Academies of Sciences, Engineering, and Medicine (NASEM). This group worked to compile the results of over ten thousand different studies on the topic, and it showed that the science remains quite limited. That's to say, no conclusive claims can be made about the short- and long-term impacts of cannabis use.

But that 2017 report *did* find substantial evidence to support a small selection of health risks and benefits. For example, there's substantial evidence demonstrating an association between cannabis use and the onset of schizophrenia or other psychoses, which are types of illnesses that cause one to lose touch with reality through experiences of delusions and hallucinations. That relationship is still complicated, however, because it doesn't necessarily say that cannabis *causes* psychotic illness. There could be other underlying vulnerabilities, such as genetic susceptibility—meaning that somebody has biological risk factors that they were born with—or that they experience other environmental vulnerabilities or risks, such as having limited access to health care or facing challenges in getting proper nutrition, those kinds of things.

Health Effects

The question is what came first, the chicken or the egg? [Is it causation (in which one factor causes another) or correlation (in which two factors are related to each other)?] In this case, is the onset of schizophrenia resulting from the use of cannabis? Or is cannabis used to deal with the symptoms of a psychotic illness, to manage the symptoms and the stresses that accompany this mental health condition? I think there is a lot of hope with the legalization of cannabis—here in Canada, certainly—that this will allow us to be able to generate more conclusive research in the area.

Addiction

This is a disorder that causes a person to have trouble controlling their drug use, even if it's causing bad things to happen, according to the National Institute on Drug Abuse.

Other health effects have also been linked to cannabis use. (Again, these are all risks for which there is substantial evidence.) There is an association, or relationship, between cannabis use and motor vehicle accidents, due to impairment caused by the drug. It is associated with low birth weight among the children of people who use cannabis during pregnancy. It's associated with a number of respiratory illnesses, such as chronic bronchitis, particularly when use is heavier and long-term. And certainly, there's quite a bit of evidence that when people initiate cannabis use young, or use it frequently, they're much more likely to use the drug in ways that lead to harm, or to develop cannabis use disorder [this term refers to cannabis addiction, or the inability to stop using cannabis even when it's messing with our physical or mental health or another factor in our lives].

But it's important to point out here, especially given the significant fear within the general public about this topic, that most people who use cannabis do so infrequently and don't experience harm. Let me reframe that: the frequency of problematic use that leads to harm is actually quite low for young people. Use tends to peak in adolescence and early adulthood, and then tapers off as people age. So we kind of expect that we will see young people who are using cannabis, experimenting with it, using it socially, those types of things. But in most cases, there aren't necessarily reasons to fear long-term impacts.

The individuals who do use cannabis in ways that result in harm tend to be concentrated within populations of young people who experience other significant, adverse life experiences—things like poverty, discrimination, exclusion, and violence. I want to underline that, because our efforts as a society should be focused on addressing these social and structural inequities if we want to minimize the challenges associated with cannabis use.

But as I mentioned, there is increased risk when cannabis use starts early and is frequent. And so at an individual level, I think we want to be targeting our intervention efforts on trying to reduce that early-onset, frequent use, to minimize the harms that can accompany cannabis.

The research I'm familiar with on teens and cannabis is largely focused in the area of cognitive function. And again, the research is really inconclusive. The health impacts that I already outlined are the only ones where we have good quality and substantial evidence to suggest that there's an association with cannabis use.

Benefits of Cannabis for Young People?

In our program of research, the Teens Report on Adolescent Cannabis Experiences (or TRACE studies), we have found that young people use cannabis for a variety of reasons. For example, some use it as a way to cope with difficult emotions, to manage stress, to fit in with peers. Some have described using cannabis to get in touch with nature and to have fun—those kinds of things. There's also evidence in the report from NASEM on the medical benefits of cannabis for young people. These include the fact that cannabis is helpful for youth in the treatment of chronic pain, and that it can be used as an antiemetic, which means it helps people who are feeling nausea or vomiting, specifically in relation to cancer treatment. There's substantial evidence documenting its effectiveness in treating muscle spasms associated with multiple sclerosis.

But beyond these effects, there are also impacts related to the legal status of cannabis, or the criminalization of youth substance use.

In situations where young people are criminally charged for things like simple possession, there can be significant adverse impacts on their future ability to achieve meaningful employment, or on other opportunities that allow them to reach their full potential.

The Risks of *Not* Talking about Weed

Unfortunately, our culture has a fear-based narrative surrounding cannabis use, particularly cannabis use by young people. It's to the point where it has shut down opportunities for the kinds of discussions where a person can ask how safe their current relationship with cannabis is. And that in and of itself creates risk for harms.

Not talking about teen cannabis use creates risk because it limits opportunities for a young person to ask a question or even to tell adults in their lives that they are using cannabis at all. That means that if teens start to experience problematic patterns of cannabis use, they often feel like there's nobody they can trust to approach and to seek help and guidance. It also means that adults modeling healthy relationships with substances can't happen, because that conversation is too taboo.

Spectrum of Use

The fact that people often don't know how to make space for those conversations is why we developed "Cycles," a video and curriculum exploring young peoples' relationships with cannabis in their everyday contexts.

The intention of the film was to create opportunities for discussion about cannabis use. It aims to be really inclusive and speak to young people about the full spectrum of use, which is another really important concept to touch on, and one that I think is largely absent from the cannabis education that's presently available. The spectrum of use is a way of understanding psychoactive substance use as occurring across a range of intensities. On one end of the spectrum is beneficial use—which is use that would be associated with positive health benefits or medicinal or spiritual purposes. Moving across the spectrum, you would then find casual or non-problematic use, which is what we would call occasional use that has negligible health or social effects. This is where most youth cannabis use would lie. Then there's problematic use, where we begin to see negative consequences for the individual, including in their social relationships. The far side of the spectrum is chronic dependence, which refers to use that has become more habitual or compulsive, despite negative health and social effects.

Most people will be on that nonproblematic end of the spectrum when it comes to using cannabis. In those cases, I wouldn't anticipate that there would be harms associated with it. I think that it's important that young people understand the concept of the spectrum of use, so that they can gauge where they are on that spectrum and recognize when they might be moving into territory that is associated with harms and seek help. I also think it's really important for the adults who have young people in their lives to be aware of the spectrum as well, because there's a lot of messaging in current cannabis educational materials that suggests that even the occasional joint with a friend is going to result in a psychotic illness, chronic dependence, or criminalization [being arrested or incarcerated]. To be able to recognize that those results are not the norm, and to create space for open dialogue, questions, support—I think that is really critical.

How Did I Get to This Work?

I don't know, I kind of landed here! I always tell people I mentor that if you remain open and try to create space for opportunities to arrive, they may lead you down a path that you didn't originally anticipate. I started off as a youth recreation worker when I was eighteen or nineteen, at a youth center adjacent to a skateboard park where I grew up hanging out. The young people who came to the center were still very much my peer community, but I was now working in a role where I was trying to respond to the negative stigma that surrounded populations of young people, including those who use drugs.

Then I ended up pursuing nursing education. I became a registered nurse, which was very much influenced by my family circumstances, which included significant mental health challenges. I was seeing that from a young age and wanted to be able to help. I ended up working in acute mental health settings, where I was embedded within a context where many people were also experiencing harms related to substance use. But I saw that the system didn't truly serve the people who we said we were there to help or support.

So I left clinical practice and went into more of a public health–oriented area of research, ultimately pursuing doctoral education to gain the skills to lead research that would allow me to help change systems, to reduce harm for people who use drugs or experience mental health challenges. I think we can have the greatest impact in our work by focusing "upstream," on the root causes of harm, whether they be discrimination, exclusion, stigma, those types of issues. And we need to work with young people—that is critical. With young people, we can help to support the building of strengths and capacities and abilities to understand evidence and to make informed decisions about the substances we use. This also helps to ensure that the research evidence we are generating is relevant and responds to the issues and information needs of youth themselves.

Understanding Young People's Real Experiences

We've made significant efforts to overcome one of the big barriers in this area of study, which is that historically, understandings about young people and substance use have never been grounded

Additional Resources on Reefer

Helpful, science-based information on cannabis designed for young adults can be hard to come by. If you want to learn more, here are some phenomenal publications and organizations:

- AsapSCIENCE YouTube channel
  https://www.youtube.com/c/AsapSCIENCE
  /search?query=cannabis
- Canadian Students for Sensible Drug Policy's *Sensible Cannabis Education* tool kit
  https://getsensible.org
- "Cycles" educational film by the University of British Columbia School of Nursing
  https://vimeo.com/275288448/5e9020e26e
- Drug Policy Alliance's "Safety First" curriculum
  https://drugpolicy.org/resource/safety-first-real-drug
  -education-teens
- *Teen Vogue*'s cannabis-related content
  https://www.teenvogue.com/tag/cannabis

in young people's experiences. One study that really stands out for me involved interviews with eighty-six young people from three communities in British Columbia, Canada—one urban, one suburban, and one rural. Across these very diverse contexts, what came through was young peoples' preference for education about substance use that is grounded in principles of harm reduction. Harm reduction is an approach to substance use that recognizes the spectrum of use that we already spoke about. The intention of harm reduction–based education is not to have young people refrain from all use but rather to try to minimize the harms associated with use.

The predominant approach to drug education has been abstinence-based and fear-based for many decades. And that is associated with harm itself, in the sense that it cuts off or limits the opportunities for young people to experience modeling of healthy substance-use practices, as well as opportunities for seeking help when their substance use is identified as leading to harm. Across these very diverse community contexts, a harm reduction approach resonated widely with young people, which was a bit surprising in the sense that some of these [communities] were quite conservative in their values.

This was a really helpful finding, actually, as it provides evidence suggesting that it may be possible to successfully implement harm reduction approaches in places where "moral" perspectives on substance use remain strong.

We want to create spaces where youth can trust adults to engage in discussions about substance use, no matter where they fall along the spectrum of use—whether they're using or not using, or whether or not they are experiencing challenges with their use. Young people need to be met with an open and non-judgmental attitude and a curiosity that allows for co-exploration of the issues—because as adults, we don't know everything about these substances either! There's lots of opportunity when a young person seeks out an adult for them to explore information and solutions together.

CHAPTER 2
Medicine

Alejo Schroeter, Fourteen-Year-Old Medicinal Marijuana Patient and His Mom, Mariana Ríos

Some young people need to say yes to medicinal uses of cannabis to live happy and healthy lives. Alejo Schroeter lives in La Plata, near Buenos Aires, Argentina. An accident at birth caused parts of his brain to become paralyzed. That trauma left him with cerebellar ataxia. The symptoms include a loss of physical coordination—in his case, uncontrollable movement of his head and arms. He also had digestive issues, vomiting, and an attention deficit disorder that made both personal relationships and schoolwork tough for him to manage. Alejo's symptoms weren't getting any better with the treatments recommended by his doctors, and his mom, Mariana Ríos, was desperate for any safe medicine that could help him.

Ríos's search brought her to medical cannabis, just as similar searches have for families around the world. Young people with severe health conditions and their loved ones have been a major driving force in legalizing medicinal marijuana. Cannabis can make dramatic improvements in the symptoms of many health conditions that affect children and teenagers, including epilepsy (which causes severe seizures), autism, and some movement disorders.

People listen when a formerly scary drug is shown to improve young peoples' lives. These kids and their families have gone

Alejo Schroeter with one of his family's cannabis plants

public with tough-to-manage diagnoses, hoping to make cannabis medicine available to everyone who needs it.

Examples of young medical marijuana patients turned activists are numerous. When she was eight years old, Grace Elizalde
received Mexico's first permission to import medicinal cannabis
products to treat her epilepsy. Colorado's Charlotte Figi was only
five when she became the United States' most recognizable advocate for CBD, a medicine that drastically reduced the number of
seizures caused by her Dravet syndrome. At the time this book
went to press, cannabis was still illegal for all uses in Bolivia. But
in 2021, the family of a five-year-old girl with spastic cerebral
palsy became the first in that country to receive permission to
import cannabis-based medicine.

The fight for access to medicinal marijuana is far from over,
and there is much debate over whether people should be able to
cultivate and process their own drugs or must rely on pharmaceuticals. In Argentina, access to medicinal cannabis has been

legalized for qualified patients. Alejo and Ríos grow his medicinal plants in their home (a 2020 law allows at-home cannabis cultivation by patients). Details of Alejo's treatment are still not approved by the government, which will not grant cultivation licenses to state employees in the federal agency where Ríos works. But Alejo and Ríos share their story with whomever they can, hoping that someday people won't need to battle health authorities for the right to access their medicine.

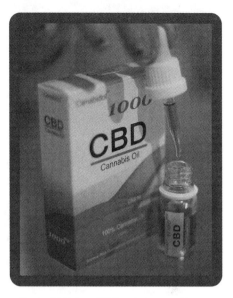

Cannabidiol, or CBD, can be used to treat seizures, anxiety, pain, Parkinson's disease, Crohn's disease, and other conditions. However, it is still illegal or heavily regulated in many places.

ALEJO SCHROETER

This Medicine Has Been Very Good for Me

I've been taking medicinal cannabis oil drops for five years. They taste a little like beer.

I started taking it because I have cerebellar ataxia. I moved my head and arms a lot. I was very tense. When I started taking it, I was able to hold my arms down, and I felt better. Before the treatment, I had to go down stairs sitting down, and now I go down them walking.

I know this medicine isn't legal for many people, and I don't know why. It's been very good for me, and it's very good at treating different kinds of diagnoses, so that you don't have the same kind of symptoms anymore.

My classmates know that I take medicinal cannabis. I sent my friend a photo of myself hugging a cannabis plant.

Sometimes my mom brings me to events about cannabis benefits. I have spoken about my story, my experience with the cannabis oil.

We have cannabis plants at home, upstairs, indoors, and also on a patio. I hug them, so that they are OK.

MARIANA RÍOS

Not a Single Death from Cannabis Overdose

In 2017, which was before the legalization of medicinal marijuana in Argentina, there was a big campaign to get the message out [about the drug's benefits], so you were always seeing videos of people on social media and on television whose health conditions had gotten much better from their cannabis treatment. One of those videos was of a patient with Parkinson's who had involuntary movements that were very similar to what Alejo was experiencing because of his cerebellar ataxia. A bell went off in my head. I started investigating, and I discovered that cannabis had worked for individuals with conditions similar to Alejo's. I also discovered that there has never been a single death from cannabis overdose, in the thousands of years in which it has been used by humans, and that its potential side effects are minimal and temporary. So, with all of that information, I decided to try the cannabis treatment on my son.

I asked everyone I knew if they knew a doctor who worked with cannabis or if they knew someone who would sell me cannabis oil, because I thought that that was how you bought it, like any other medicinal product. I couldn't find a doctor. I did find a cultivator who was in solidarity with us, and who, without even knowing me, made an appointment to meet up with me clandestinely, on a street corner. It was as if she was a drug trafficker and I was a drug addict. She also gave me flowers from the same cannabis plant that the oil was made from, and a [living] cannabis plant. Plus, she taught me how to make the oil for my son, because the only way I could get more was to cultivate it ourselves.

My Own Experience with Cannabis

I tried it when I was twenty years old, and it didn't seem like a dangerous drug. Cannabis helped me relax at night when I was ready to sleep. I realized that the kinds of lessons about cannabis they had taught us in school were lies. My own experience led me to believe that it could help my son.

This Changed Our Lives

Alejo was unable to walk before taking this medicine. He had to grab onto a wall, or be assisted by someone else, because he had zero equilibrium, due in part to the involuntary movements his head and arms made. From the day he was born and continuing until he first took medicinal cannabis when he was nine years old—every day of his life—he would vomit. He had attention deficit disorder. The involuntary movements didn't allow him to be able to read the chalkboard or speak fluidly with others. Besides that, he was having lots of digestive issues. He only had a bowel movement once a week, which caused him a lot of suffering.

Since he began consuming cannabis, Alejo doesn't just *walk* on his own—he is now able to go up and down stairs on his own. His attention deficit disorder improved, as did his social relationships with his classmates in school. His communication skills improved a lot. What can he do now that he couldn't do before? He's able to take baths, change his clothes, brush his teeth, go to bed on his own. In terms of the digestive issues, Alejo hasn't vomited in five years. He began eating food that he wouldn't eat before. His digestive system became more regular. The truth is, this changed our lives.

Being Open about Alejo's Treatment

His classmates have come to my house. They've seen the cannabis plants, and we have explained to them why Alejo takes this medicine. He's a public figure [for the medicinal marijuana movement] in my city and my country, so of course his classmates know. He has beautiful friends who really love him.

CHAPTER 3
Food That Makes You Feel Funny

Richard Villegas, Music Journalist and Cannabis
Edibles Consumer

N ot everyone who uses cannabis does so for medicinal purposes. Consuming cannabis recreationally is also a completely valid interaction with the plant! One could argue
that any use of a psychoactive substance, whether it's for
relaxing at the end of a long day or even getting so high you momen-
tarily forget about your problems, has a therapeutic purpose.

Regardless of one's motives, taking too much weed can lead
to an unpleasant situation. In my experience, most bad marijuana
trips happen after eating an edible. That's mainly because it's
impossible to tell how much THC (remember, that's the main
cannabinoid in marijuana that makes us high) is contained in a
homemade brownie, gummy, mineral water, or any other kind of
cannabis product made to be eaten or drunk. Dispensary goods,
on the other hand, must meet local rules and usually include
ingredient labels. There are also physiological reasons behind
intense edible trips. When you smoke weed, its THC enters your
bloodstream, which is not the most effective way of breaking
down the cannabinoid to reap its psychoactive effects. But when
you eat marijuana, your saliva immediately breaks up the THC.

Then it goes on to your stomach and liver. The liver converts the intoxicating cannabinoid, rendering it far more potent than the same amount of THC would have been if you'd smoked it.

What does a bad edibles high feel like? It's usually like a panic attack. Your heart rate can ratchet up, and you may have difficulty breathing or experience body temperature changes. That's in addition to symptoms such as feeling paranoid or confused, losing your physical coordination, or even throwing up. Sometimes weirder things happen. One time, after I ate a double dose of marijuana-infused ice cream in a Mexico City cannabis protest march, my eyes stopped focusing, effectively blinding me for about an hour! Not fun.

But you can do things to avoid bad trips. First, make sure you know how much THC is in your edible. Next, check that your edible doesn't contain synthetic cannabis. These chemical compounds

Cannabis dispensaries carry a variety of edibles, including beverages, baked goods, chips, gummies, and candy. Edibles sold at dispensaries must meet rules about how much THC they contain. That can really benefit consumers, who want to know what dose will match their tolerance level for THC and other cannabinoids.

are marketed under names like Spice and K2 whose effects can be quite different from legitimate cannabis. These drugs have been associated with severe health risks and even death.

Consume edibles only when you're around people you trust, in a place and time when you feel safe and can mentally check out for several hours. Don't eat more if you don't feel high "enough" right away—you may not feel the effects until one to two hours after consuming an edible. Again, that's because of the THC's detour through the stomach and liver, compared with the quick entry into your bloodstream that happens when you smoke marijuana or consume it using a vaporizer. (Cannabis concentrates, like those used in vape pens, can also pack an unexpected punch.)

If you do eat too much weed, get to a secure, calm location. Lie down if you can, and focus on taking deep breaths to relax. Try eating something without marijuana in it, and drink a glass of water. Taking a few drops of CBD oil or gnawing on a black peppercorn are other folk remedies that some people use to bring them back to earth. The main thing is to remember that these symptoms will be gone in a few hours. Most of these tips will work regardless of how you ingested weed!

If you want to learn more about responsible and even non-psychoactive weed-eating—which human beings have likely been practicing since the early Neolithic period—check out chapter 6.

I asked my dear friend, the Colombian–Puerto Rican music journalist Richard Villegas, who was raised in the United States and the Dominican Republic (check out his podcast *Songmess* if you're into indie music from across Latin America!), to share his first experience of eating THC-infused cannabis food as a teen in Buenos Aires, Argentina. I wanted to include his debut edibles story because the trip had bad and good moments—and because he's had ample time to reflect on the simple things he and his friends could have done to make their cannabis voyage a lot more chill.

RICHARD VILLEGAS

My First Edibles Trip: Where and Why

I was nineteen and living in Buenos Aires—I had gotten there two, three months prior. And motivation? I wanted to get high! I wanted to party, I wanted to have a good time. Buenos Aires is a big party city. There was a lot of clubbing, a lot of night-life. And weed—well, there was a big hippie culture in Buenos Aires. Lots of handmade things, and weed was pretty common. I knew a lot of people who smoked it, but I had only had mild experiences, like contact highs. I don't think I smoked cannabis until I was in my mid-twenties, because my parents were very antidrug and they kind of put the fear of God into me. But yeah, for my first experience with edibles, I got

Richard Villegas, music writer

together with my friend Sarah, who is from Portland, and her roommate, this other guy whose name I don't remember, who was from Boston.

Sarah and her roommate had this brick of weed [in South America, cheap weed comes pressed into blocks—they call it prensado], and it was kind of old. They were even wondering if it was still good. The idea was to cook it—we had the idea to make a cake. We went to the supermarket and bought some cheap wine to drink, a Pepperidge Farm-type cake mix, frosting, and we were like, OK, let's make a cake! They were definitely more adept at marijuana consumption, so they knew that they needed to fry it in butter, to, I guess, get the essence of the marijuana out? As far as I understand, they were supposed to have strained out the weed bits, but they never did. They just threw it all in the mix, twigs and seeds and all. [Another author's note: Richard's right—when making weed butter, you definitely want to strain out these parts!] We put it in the oven, and then we started drinking. I had an entire bottle of wine.

Drinking that much did not improve the experience at all, because it makes it harder to control, or to calibrate. I think you need to choose to do one or the other. Again, I'm an adult now— I'm thirty-four—and I generally prefer to drink than to consume any other sort of drug, but the only times I ever feel like the buzz gets out of my hands or that I might throw up is whenever I mix alcohol with weed. I would advise that those experiences be kept separate, or at least, if you're going to drink alcohol while smoking, drink very little.

I don't know exactly how much weed we used. They were grinding it up, and I remember asking, "So roughly, how many joints can we roll with this?" And they said, "About five." Mind you, it was a small tin of cake that in hindsight turned out to be quite potent!

It did not taste good! It tasted like weed, and I don't really enjoy the taste of weed. We just smothered it in frosting and then chugged some wine along with it.

What Happened Next

We were all getting a little impatient. My friends, who were weed smokers, were used to a more immediate high, and I was certainly impatient. I was like, "Girl, where is the weed? Where's the high? I'm trying to fly." And it would not come, so I just kept drinking wine. I was like, "I'm going to get this buzz one way or another." [laughs] I had another piece of cake . . . and then an hour later, the tingles started. We all started getting giggly and lightheaded. I distinctly remember making, like, funny observations, and then I stumbled onto a book of Beat poetry. Don't ask me who it was by—[Jack] Kerouac, maybe, but it wasn't *On the Road*. Whatever it was, it was very rant-driven with page-long sentences—run-on, kind of stream-of-consciousness type of thing. The Boston guy, he was telling me that it was a very intense book, or whatever. So I started reading a random page and ended up falling into the rhythm of the poetry. As I read it—performed it, I guess—my two friends kind of got into the rhythm too, and we started swaying back and forth. At one point the Boston guy was like, "You need to stop. I'm starting to freak out." And then we chilled out for a bit longer.

Not Completely Enjoyable

Well, it definitely felt like a ton of bricks had just dropped on me when the high finally hit. By hour two, I was melting—which was not necessarily unpleasant. But then I was like, "OK, this is getting overwhelming. I'm going to go home and I'm going to lie down." I went outside and hailed a taxi. This was pre-Uber, and taxis in Buenos Aires were very common. I got in the cab and was making casual banter with the driver. But then the driver started taking me by a route that I did not recognize, and in my highness I started to freak out a little bit. I was like, "Oh my God, I'm getting kidnapped. I'm getting kidnapped in Argentina." My thoughts started running wildly. And then suddenly we stopped, and the driver was like, "You're here." And it was my building, and I went home and passed out.

All in all, my experience was not so bad. But I checked in with my friend Sarah the next morning and she told me that she had a panic attack. She went to bed shortly after I left and closed the door and lay in bed. But she could see the light underneath the door, and shadows of all these people, and she started to think that the shadows were, like, some otherworldly entity that was coming for her. And the Boston guy, he drank and ate a lot more, and apparently, he had a crazy experience. He really started to freak out, and I believe he vomited. Eventually, everybody just crashed.

My Cannabis Use Today

I don't use it too much because I find that it's a big time commitment. Whenever I consume it, the rest of my day is shot—I'm not able to work or engage in many social situations. My conversation skills and my short-term memory disappear. But I do use it for my mental health. I'm a music journalist, and I spend a lot of time writing and in very social situations. I carry a lot of anxiety, and I'm often thinking about twenty things at the same time. Edibles help me reboot my brain. It's like when you turn your phone off and on again—it's suddenly faster, brighter. It's like, boom! You're more present. It's almost like brushing your teeth, but brushing your brain. It feels tingly and minty fresh, and it really is marvelous.

When I do eat edibles, I want to experience a bit of the high. I usually take one so that I can watch shows or a movie or something. I want to have weird moments. I want to laugh. I watch a lot of comedy stuff, whether it's a movie, show, or YouTube video, or whatever. I was watching [YouTuber] Jeffree Star review a makeup palette recently and I was cackling. You know, just laughing at completely nonsense things. And then I have a much more pleasant sleeping experience.

Reflecting on My First Edibles Experience

I wouldn't change a thing, honestly. Thankfully, we were all good and safe afterwards, although I did feel a little paranoid for a

CHAPTER 4
Underground Education

Polita Pepper, Cultivator and Educator

Because of criminal penalties and the stigma of prohibited psychoactive substances, traditional educational organizations such as colleges, universities, and governmental agencies haven't provided much education about marijuana in the modern era. Peoples' unmet needs for knowledge about the plant has given birth to a global network of cannabis educators who empower others in talks, workshops, and courses. In Oakland, California, Oaksterdam declared itself the first cannabis university when it opened in 2007, when recreational marijuana was still illegal in the state. Oaksterdam offers classes in cultivation, extraction, and cannabis business operation. In places with legalized cannabis, educational options sponsored by traditionally accredited institutions are finally starting to pop up. In the United States, more than thirty universities offer courses in marijuana-related subjects, from a University of Maryland master's program in medical cannabis science and therapeutics to six-month certification courses at Syracuse University in everything from cannabis law to horticulture. Cannabis teachers have honed their knowledge despite law enforcement's persecution of their industry and promoted time-tested methods of self-care.

Oaksterdam University offers educational training related to the cannabis industry, including courses on cultivation, manufacturing, public policy, and business strategy.

In Mexico City, the educational organization Cannativa offers classes on cannabis medicine and the plant's other usages. The group was founded in 2014 by Mexican anthropologist Polita Pepper and Brazilian journalist Nico Malazarte. They had just returned from learning cultivation techniques on organic Northern California cannabis farms and were acutely aware of the need for information regarding medicinal marijuana in prohibition-era Mexico. The duo started Cannativa as a series of sporadic and highly clandestine cultivation intensives in Mexico City before Mexico's 2017 legalization of medicinal marijuana. Their first students were largely older women, caretakers of medicinal cannabis patients. But eventually the courses attracted a diverse student body, including medical professionals interested in the benefits of the drug.

The project has grown to a catalog of thirty courses that range from how to make a medicinal marijuana extract to cannabis cultivation for women to a 101 on effective and accurate journalism about drugs. Limited legalization of medicinal cannabis in Mexico has not made their educational mission any less urgent. The only products that the country has legalized for widespread medicinal use are CBD-based cannabis pharmaceuticals. Government agents see them as less risky for patients due to stringent testing protocols. But legal products don't include the THC that many patients need to treat their symptoms. Large international corporations usually produce the legal pharmaceuticals with costly price tags. Those are often too expensive for the average Mexican family—especially when compared with the price of growing and processing your own weed.

Cannativa's work in helping consumers and producers understand the science of cannabis is also important in the context of the country's legalization movement, which goes beyond the plant's medical uses. Mainstream Mexican media loves its stigmatizing and fictitious portrayals of cannabis. For example, in a 2017 episode of the long-running Catholic TV series *La Rosa de Guadalupe*, a young cook's little sister is unable to wake up after accidentally eating the marijuana brownies her sibling cooked for friends. The girl is taken to the hospital to have her stomach pumped. This is rarely, if ever, necessary for people who eat too much weed.

As part of her mission to combat misinformation, Cannativa cofounder Polita Pepper regularly travels to other countries to lecture on cannabis issues—and to judge competitions of weed grown by local cultivators. At the time of our interview, she was working on a dissertation outlining the roles that cannabis plays in communities of Indigenous campesinos (farmers in Mexico whose families come from the lands they work) who have been growing cannabis for generations. Her research frames the drug as a longstanding national cultural tradition, rather than fodder for media-exaggerated criminal psychosis. Pepper is dedicated to gender justice within the industry, and in 2020 she directed a short film for Cannativa called "Jardín de Hembras" [Garden of Women] that explores trans identity through the lens of cannabis cultivation. She's also the cofounder of the Latin American Network of Women in Cannabis. In 2021 it released *Cannábicas*, a documentary that features the experiences of two hundred women in thirty countries who work in the weed industry.

POLITA PEPPER

A Community of People Who Needed Hope

Nico and I had just come back to Mexico after working on medicinal cannabis farms in California. Because cannabis was not legal in Mexico, getting access to it as a medicine was very hard. Since many families needed to learn how to grow their own for their sick kids, we decided to teach the people "how to fish," instead of "selling them fish." At the beginning, our project didn't have a name, we weren't very established, and most of the people who came to our workshops were the parents of kids with very complex diseases who had been diagnosed as terminal cases. These were people who had tried absolutely every kind of treatment and medica-

Polita Pepper, cofounder of Cannativa

tion to help their children, and who had discovered that medicinal marijuana could offer them a small window that gave them hope. That's how Cannativa began, with a community of people who needed hope. It has grown into something that gives these people a reason to exist. We want the education we provide to be the tool that allows these families—these mothers, these children, these grandparents—the ability to make the basic elements for their medicine in their own homes and gardens, a possibility to live in a way that the traditional medical system does not offer.

Many of the people who come to the Cannativa courses have never even seen a cannabis plant, so they have no way of knowing the parameters of what makes a quality cannabis medicine. [If they weren't learning about quality cannabis through Cannativa], they could wind up buying products of bad quality. That could put their families' health at risk—and that's what led them to search for cannabis in the first place.

Cannativa's Classes

When we first began—wow, those classes were beautiful. We would pick a meeting point in front of a subway station because we couldn't tell people the address of the classes for security reasons. At that point, it was too dangerous. We'd load everyone into a '94 Ford Econoline van and drive them to the workshop location, where we'd spend six to eight hours learning about how to grow cannabis and make medicinal extractions from it. With time, we learned that less was more—that giving people too much information at once made it too difficult to process. So as the years went by, we started picking out the basic content that would satisfy the educational needs of our students. Today, eight years later, Cannativa has courses that range from beginning level to specialized offerings—thirty different classes in total.

Celebrating Our Students

[I have] so many stories! But there was the case of Pau, an excellent illustrator who was diagnosed at twenty-three years old with a very aggressive form of cancer. She was young, enthusiastic, and already a cannabis consumer when she signed up for her first Cannativa course a year later. She took that first class with her mom. For the next three years, she effectively treated the symptoms of her cancer with cannabis. She didn't survive. But she was able to transform the attitudes of her family to the point that they themselves started cultivating cannabis, and they're still active in cannabis to this day.

I think it's important to celebrate the stories of people who are no longer with us—and not just because they were warriors and we honor them through their memory. But also because sometimes improving the quality of life of someone fighting a disease as terrible as cancer . . . maybe this medicine doesn't make their life *longer*, but it can change the quality of the time that they have left. Pau died when she was twenty-seven years old, super young, but the last three years of her life were radically different for her and her family. During that time, they participated in so much activism around cannabis issues—the medicine transformed their family. They would walk in the cannabis rights protest marches here in Mexico City. Pau would be photographed protesting in her wheelchair. To this day, her mother, grandmother, and aunt have cannabis businesses in honor of her. The medicine was supposed to be for her, but really, it transformed the whole family.

Legalization Doesn't Guarantee Access

The legalization of medicinal cannabis in Mexico has been a very elitist process that does not ensure financial access to these products for all the Mexicans who need it. In addition, the investigation the government has conducted is insufficient—there are more than one hundred cannabinoids, all of them have therapeutic properties, and the medicinal regulation we have only focuses on one of these, CBD!

I think that education around this issue will always be important. It's a tool for social transformation. Legalization is just a governmental framework—it does not always guarantee access to quality medicine. We have to educate not only cannabis consumers but also cannabis businesses. We need to establish quality control for products. The fact that cannabis is legal doesn't prevent cannabis businesses from [using] misleading publicity and marketing—in Mexico, you can already see that happening with CBD products.

Cannabis users need certain information. What is cannabis? How does one use it? What products are appropriate for me? What kinds of health conditions can cannabis treat? What kinds of products are not safe to consume? What kinds of questions do I need to ask my cannabis provider to know that they are selling trustworthy products? What kinds of questions do I need to ask my health-care provider about cannabis? None of these answers are guaranteed by legalization—but we need to know about them for our own self-care.

Cultivate Yourself

Self-cultivation is, in very simple terms, a relationship generated between oneself and the cannabis plant. In that relationship, you watch your medicine grow. The act of making oneself responsible for the quality of the final product is only going to make you more conscious of everything that goes into your medication.

Beyond that, I think self-cultivation is a therapeutic exercise—a concept that is very interesting to explore when we're talking about patients of terminal health conditions. It's an act of emancipation that allows us to transform our own lives, listen to our minds work, grow the possibilities of existing in this world.

CHAPTER 5
A Tool for Athletes
Al Harrington, Former NBA Player and Entrepreneur

Pro athletes regularly endure high-impact collisions and life-changing physical trauma while they're on the clock—common sources of injuries whose symptoms can be helped by cannabis. Some of the most publicized cases of famous people getting in trouble for marijuana-related offenses involve sports stars of color. That's nothing new: celebrities of color have served as the targets of drug police since jazz great Louis Armstrong became the first famous person arrested for cannabis possession in the United States in 1930.

Al Harrington knows all about the limits placed on athletes for cannabis use. The New Jersey–born basketball forward was drafted out of high school and played for sixteen seasons. But during his final years in the National Basketball Association (NBA), a major knee injury left Harrington in a world of hurt. Team doctors prescribed addictive painkillers—drugs that can cause fatigue and loss of concentration, among other health conditions—but Harrington had another plan. He began taking cannabis-derived CBD. It gave him non-habit-forming pain relief and inspired in him a deep and lasting respect for the medicinal powers of cannabis. At the time, the NBA did not allow its players to use the plant in any form. Harrington had to keep his medicine secret from league officials to avoid costly fines and game suspensions.

Because of zero-tolerance marijuana policies, athletes from

nearly every pro league—again, most of them people of color— have had their games, salaries, and lives publicly derailed over their use of cannabis. The problems are so severe that in 2016, a group of athletes founded an advocacy group called Athletes for Care. Their website lists nearly 150 influential athlete ambassadors, including Harrington, who speak on the importance of cannabis access in improving health and safety for athletes.

Weed entrepreneur Al Harrington

Harrington once estimated that 80 percent of players use cannabis. He doesn't want them to have to choose between following the rules and taking care of their well-being. In 2011, four years before Harrington's retirement from the NBA, he founded the cannabis company Viola, which also runs an investment fund focused on supporting Black entrepreneurs. In the cannabis industry, less than 2 percent of business owners are Black. The brand is named after Harrington's grandmother, whose vision-impairing glaucoma symptoms were so alleviated by cannabis that she was able to read her beloved Bible again.

The advocacy of pros-gone-cannabis-entrepreneurs have likely helped to shift how professional sports leagues treat cannabis use. They include Harrington, fellow NBA alum Shawn Kemp, former football running back Ricky Williams, and ex-Women's National Basketball Association (WNBA) player Sue Bird. The National Hockey League has removed penalties for positive THC tests and treats them as a health issue. The National Football League (NFL) allows players to consume cannabis in the off-season and has announced a million-dollar research investment in studies on the role CBD could play in managing players' pain and protecting their brains from concussions. The National Women's Soccer League allows players to take CBD. Major League Baseball took cannabis off its list of banned substances in 2019. While the WNBA continues to test and punish for cannabis use, in 2021 the NBA chose to continue its temporary halt on random marijuana testing.

Harrington talked to me about why these changes have been a long time coming.

AL HARRINGTON

Guilt by Association

When [I was young] my grandmother would overreact to my uncle for coming out smelling like reefer. She'd go crazy, cuss him out, and sometimes kick him out of the house for smoking. And then there was the police side of it. When I was between eight and ten years old, I was starting to get that freedom where I could kind of go wherever I wanted, in regards to staying outside and hanging out. We'd be outside at the corner store called John's Deli, and the police would pull up on us, make everybody get up against the wall, and go through everybody's pockets. Nobody had anything on them, it was all for—what? You know what I'm saying? And I was one of those kids, trying to deal with guilt by association, and that was something we felt a lot where I grew up.

Cannabis Is Kind of Our Drug

I honestly believe that cannabis is kind of our drug, meaning Black people. I think it's something that we like to use. I think it's just the way it makes you feel. It's something that kind of mellows you out. Obviously, I think that people use cannabis for medicinal reasons, but they were more aware at the time of going to the doctor's [to] get [non-cannabis] prescriptions. But different shit that you were dealing with, whether it's anxiety or depression, or different things like that, people then would use cannabis to deal with that.

NFL players especially will use it to make their bodies feel better, all their aches and pains. But when there's a stigma attached to [that], you can't even have these conversations. I feel like that's one of the big benefits that people get from it, is the pain relief.

I'll be honest, I was kind of ignorant to the facts [about cannabis when I was a young player]. I thought that it was a gateway drug [a term used to try to discourage people from using relatively harmless substances like weed, based on the largely bogus theory that they prime consumers to try more addictive drugs] most of my career. Eighteen straight years of my life, people were telling me that it was bad for you. Now you look at it, and you realize all the benefits from it. [At Viola] we're going to keep pushing the envelope, and we want it to be readily available to all athletes.

Medicating Safely

In 2012, I had a botched knee surgery. That's when I started taking cannabis to deal with my pain, instead of taking all those pills that they gave me. I mean, honestly, between the years of '02 to '09 I took three Celebrex a day to deal with the inflammation I was having in my body. I was debating it in my mind, knowing all the side effects. But I had no choice, no other options, so I had to get to the end of my career to realize that I could have been medicating safely, essentially, without all these side effects. You know, I think that's what really drives me to push this forward, to try to get this medicine to all athletes across all sports.

I just dealt with [the stress]. I didn't smoke in season. I just used CBD products. That's when I realized that [the NBA] obviously does not test for CBD. They really only test for THC, you know what I'm saying? They say we can't use any cannabis or its by-products. But they only test for THC.

I've Got a Voice

Things kept happening, dominoes kept falling, which just opened up this door for me that I never thought would open. I remember going to different meetings with billionaires, real estate investors, and we talked about being interested in figuring out cannabis. A little while after I had these conversations, I just realized that like, damn, I've got a voice. I've got a platform that nobody else in the state has. It happened kind of naturally. This was not something that I set out to do. I just got more and more of an education. I think that's the main thing about it: without the education, I would have never done it. But I was educating myself, slowly but surely, to the point where I realized that this is something that has to happen. Like, there was no other option.

Changing the NBA's Policy

Honestly, for me it was really about telling [former NBA commissioner David Stern] why I was using [cannabis], and then the typical scenario of an athlete, right? We train our bodies for close to six hours, but we only play thirty minutes of the game, and then we've got to come down. And for a lot of people, they're dealing with issues, or they're dealing with pain, or whatever. A lot of times, you'd turn to alcohol to calm your body down, different things like that. But all that does is leave you dehydrated and hungover the next day, right? Then you have the pharmaceutical drugs, same thing. You know, they talk about making sure that we don't abuse those drugs. Well, if you don't introduce them to us, then we don't have to! We know that pharmaceutical drugs are addictive—they're highly addictive. So I talked to [Stern] in layman's terms, being very specific and being simplistic about the approach. All leagues after that—not just the NBA—they started to really change the way that cannabis was perceived.

Making the Industry More Equitable

We've got to continue to create opportunities in regards to [cannabis business] licensing [for Black entrepreneurs] because the licensing has a lot of value, obviously. The next level is to address the resources that are attached to it because they are very central to this business. If it's your first time in the business, you're going to have screwups, and they're costly. If you don't have proper resources, one screwup and you lose your business, you know what I'm saying? I've had twenty [screwups], right? And if I didn't have the resources I had, I wouldn't have this business; we wouldn't be [having this conversation].

At one point, I thought the industry should support the industry, in regards to multistate operators and stuff like that, that it should provide funds [to Black entrepreneurs]. But that's really difficult because of the way the tax structure is geared around cannabis—legal cannabis is not as lucrative as a lot of people think! The one who is making the money is the government, with all this tax money. I feel like they're the ones who should be giving back and making the initial investments in social equity applicants [author's note: this term refers to entrepreneurs who are eligible for state programs that give cannabis business licensing priority to people who have been impacted by the War on Drugs], until they get up and running. I think New York is one of the states that is going to try to do that, and I'm pulling for them that they're successful. Because if it is, I think that's the way that people of color will be really able to benefit from the industry.

Cannabis Justice

I think that cannabis justice is really about freeing the plant, allowing it to be federally legal, so that we can build a real industry, just like liquor and the lottery. Free the plant!

United States Athletes and Teams Singled Out by Cannabis Prohibition

Portland Trail Blazers: Portland, Oregon, has one of the highest rates of weed dispensaries to people in the United States. But years ago, it was not cool with the cannabis consumption of its NBA team. Between November 2004 and January 2005, three Trail Blazers were charged or cited for misdemeanor cannabis possession, including point guard Damon Stoudamire. This hometown hero, who had led his Portland high school team to two state championships, became the target of intense public criticism. Months later, a newspaper columnist brought a drug test to the Blazers' practice, and an incredulous Stoudamire found himself peeing in a cup for the writer's story.

Nick Diaz: A funny thing happened in 2015 after Ultimate Fighting Championship (UFC) fighter Nick Diaz faced off against Anderson Silva. Both tested positive for banned substances. Silva was found to be taking two kinds of anabolic steroids and was suspended for a year. Diaz tested positive for cannabis for the third time since he'd been in the league and was initially suspended for *five* years. "We got a whole system trying to hold me down," he told reporters. His suspension was later reduced, but Diaz didn't make it back to the league until 2021, when the UFC removed cannabis from its list of banned substances.

His younger brother, Nate, with whom Nick founded a CBD line, has joined the campaign to normalize cannabis within the sport. Nate shook the UFC world when he vaped onstage at a prefight press conference the year after his brother was suspended. "It's CBD," he clarified. "It helps with the healing process and inflammation and stuff like that. So you wanna get these for before [and] after the fight. It'll make your life a better place."

Sha'Carri Richardson: In 2021 the twenty-one-year-old sprinter was predicted to win the Olympics gold medal in the 100-meter race. Then she tested positive for THC—in Oregon, a state where recreational weed is legal. But World Anti-Doping Agency regulations don't consider local law, and she was disqualified from running the race at the Olympics. Later, Richardson shared that her mother had died days before her positive test and that she had consumed marijuana to deal with professional pressure and the heavy emotions surrounding her loss. The incident led to a widespread questioning over how drugs are policed in pro sports. Particularly controversial was that various participating Olympians were sponsored by CBD brands—or owned one themselves, such as soccer player Megan Rapinoe.

Sha'Carri Richardson finished first in the women's 100-meter final with a time of 10.86 seconds to qualify for the Olympics on June 19, 2021.

Brittney Griner: Just before Russian forces invaded Ukraine in 2021, this two-time Olympic athlete and WNBA star—and the first openly LGBTQIA+ athlete to be endorsed by Nike—was arrested in the Moscow airport for cannabis possession. The center, who had been competing on a Russian team during the WNBA's off-season, was sentenced to nine years in prison. The United States government determined that she was wrongfully detained and after ten months was able to negotiate for her release through a prisoner swap involving a noted Russian arms dealer.

Part 2

CANNA CULTURE

CHAPTER 6
Nutritious and Delicious Eats
Joline Rivera, Food Media Professional

Hemp can be used in a dizzying number of ways, as medicine, as an ingredient in cosmetics, and as an environmentally friendly industrial material. Car manufacturer BMW has been using hemp in its car door panels for years! You'll read more about the industrial uses of the plant in the next two chapters.

People even use the plant to make food. Even though the words "cannabis edible" may bring to mind the modern weed brownie, there are records from four thousand years ago of people in South Asia eating cannabis. In India the millennia-old cannabis-milk mixture bhang is associated with the Hindu god Lord Shiva and is typically drunk during the colorful spring festival of Holi.

But the kinds of cannabis you can eat or drink are not limited to foods flush with THC. (See chapter 3 for more on eating those kinds of snacks safely.) Foods made from nonintoxicating hemp can be rich in protein, fiber, magnesium, and omega-3 fatty acids and can make everyday recipes tasty and more nutritious. If you're ready to experiment, here's some good news: kids and young adults can legally buy hulled hemp seeds (called hemp hearts), hemp milk, or hemp flour in a grocery store—unlike the infamous weed brownie. In recent years, foods have also been produced with CBD. Cannabinol is not 100 percent off-limits for kids. The first cannabis-based drug that was approved for use in the United States, Epidiolex, is a CBD-based medicine often used to treat epilepsy in young people. Talk to your pediatrician before using any product with CBD, and know that age restrictions may apply in their sale.

Chicago-based, Mexican American foodie and media professional Joline Rivera runs *Kitchen Toke*. The publication provides recipes for making different kinds of cannabis-infused foods, as well as inspiring photos of gourmet cannabis eats—like a flaky pain au chocolat pastry whose sweetness comes from a CBD-infused chocolate bar or a baking sheet of Brazilian corn truffles covered in hemp hearts. (Note: *Kitchen Toke* also features cannabis recipes with THC, and its website is not meant to be browsed by underage chefs.) Rivera is also the creator of Red Belly Honey, a brand of honey infused with CBD. In our interview, she shared her knowledge about the many reasons why people eat cannabis, in addition to some delicious recipes from *Kitchen Toke* that you can make at home.

Magazine founder Joline Rivera recognized that many people were looking for a way to ingest cannabis without smoking it, partly from her own quest for well-being.

JOLINE RIVERA

You Could Physically See the Pain Go Away

I tried cannabis in high school, but it wasn't really for me. I wasn't the type of person to go out with my friends looking for alcohol or to get high. I was really into sports then, and because there was so much partying in my family, I really tried to steer away from [drugs]. But in 2011, [my codesigner] Nellie Williams's dad was diagnosed with lung cancer. He tried every trial, test, chemo, you name it, but by 2016, he was losing his battle. He was unable to get rest. He was in pain; he wasn't eating. It was hard to sit by and watch my friend's anguish over her father. So I said to her, "What if we tried some cannabis?"

My friend Whitney and I drove from Chicago to Missouri to meet up with Nellie and deliver some high-dose THC chocolates to her dad. He tried them, and about forty-five minutes in, you could physically see the pain go away. He started to smile, and then he was like, "I want to play with the kids. I want to go outside for a walk. I'm hungry." His six daughters and wife all said that they hadn't seen [him] like that in a really long time.

One Good Day

He passed away a few weeks later. At the funeral, Nellie's whole family was coming up to me and saying, "Joline, we keep talking about how you gave our dad one good day." That stuck with me.

I thought, "There's so many people living in pain, so many people who are sick, so many people like him who don't know about cannabis. Why did it take so much time and energy for me to find information about cooking with cannabis?" Pharmaceuticals aren't the end-all, and they don't help everybody.

One day I said to Nellie, "What if we flipped everything that we've been doing for the last ten or fifteen years—the designing, creating food content, recipes, chefs, work, video, all of it—and start orienting it towards food made with cannabis?" That's how our media company *Kitchen Toke* was born. We really just set out to help someone else have just one more good day.

Nutritional Benefits of Hemp

In 2014, I was not feeling well, and even though I was training for a triathlon, I was gaining more and more weight. I had five different doctors ask me what I was eating, and when I told them, they accused me of not being honest. They insisted I had to be eating more than I was telling. It wasn't true, so I left and never returned. Finally, I met Dr. Paul Savage, who listened, took my blood, ran tests, and I learned I had insulin resistance. His instructions were a lean diet, more healthy proteins, natural sugars, and healthy fats. I really started to pay attention to how much protein I needed and discovered how complicated it was to cook for myself. I wanted foods that were quick and easy, snacks that tasted really good and didn't take much time. Hemp hearts are some of my favorite [hemp food products].

Hemp seeds are a nutritious nut with a mild flavor that can be eaten raw, cooked, or toasted.

[Hemp seeds] are a great way to access protein, which helps build muscle and makes me feel full quicker. The best part—because they're loaded with healthy fats and are natural antioxidants—is that they're also good for my skin. I don't have to deal with breakouts as much as I used to! I add hemp hearts to my after-workout smoothies. They are a nice energy boost, and that protein is needed after I leave the gym.

Healthy Hemp Recipes for Teen Cooks

From *Kitchen Toke*

Hemp Power Balls

Recipe by Laura Lagano

⅓ cup (75 g) sunflower seed butter
⅓ cup (53 g) hemp hearts
2 tablespoons (18 g) tart dried cherries, chopped
1 tablespoon (5 g) cacao
1 tablespoon (15 ml) canna oil
1 teaspoon (2 g) hemp powder
pinch kosher salt
unsweetened coconut flakes

1. In a bowl, combine all of the ingredients except the coconut flakes. Stir well to combine.
2. Using a scant tablespoon for each, roll mixture into balls. Toss with coconut flakes to coat fully. Arrange on a parchment-lined baking sheet.
3. Refrigerate until firm. Then transfer to an airtight container. Makes about 16 balls.

Hemp Granola

Recipe by Laura Yee

¾ cup (106 g) raw almonds
½ cup (75 g) raw pumpkin seeds (pepitas)
½ cup (50 g) raw pecans
1 cup (120 g) raw walnuts
1 cup (60 g) unsweetened coconut flakes
1 cup (160 g) hemp seeds
⅓ cup (78 ml) melted coconut oil
1 teaspoon (5 ml) vanilla
1 teaspoon (2 g) cinnamon
¼ cup (59 ml) maple syrup
pinch of sea salt
½ cup (88 g) pitted and chopped Medjool dates
¾ cup (108 g) golden raisins

1. Preheat oven to 250°F (120°C). Place almonds, pumpkin seeds, pecans, and walnuts into a food processor. Pulse a few times to chop the nuts and seeds into smaller pieces.
2. Transfer the nut mixture into a large bowl. Add all the remaining ingredients except the dates and raisins. Stir well. Spread an even layer of the mixture onto a large parchment-lined baking sheet.
3. Bake for 35 minutes. Remove from the oven. Add dates and raisins, and give the mix a good stir. Bake for 25 to 30 minutes more or until granola is golden brown in color. Remove it from the oven, and let it cool. The granola will harden as it cools. The cooler it gets, the crunchier it'll be. Makes 6 to 8 servings.

Foods Infused with CBD

CBD can provide quick-yet-prolonged relief from mild pains and from daily stresses and anxiety. They also help you to relax, so you can sleep easier. It's a way for anyone to enjoy the benefits of cannabis without the psychoactive experience.

Our [Red Belly Honey] bees live on a wide-open wine vineyard that also grows cannabis, just north of Santa Barbara [California]. They gather nectar and pollen from flowers around them, as well as a full spectrum hemp nectar we offer them. Bees instinctively know what they need. If you offer a sick bee a few different nectars, they gravitate to the nectar that will make them better. Bees choose this nectar, and we've seen how incredibly healthy they are because of it. They predigest it for us and create the first water-soluble CBD when they express [deposit] these cannabinoids into the honeycomb cell. We gather the honeycombs [and] spin them in a drum. The honey comes out, and we put the honeycomb back in the hives so that the bees don't have to rebuild their wax honeycombs all over again.

We Need to Support People of Color

The history of cannabis and hemp show us that people of color have been hurt and punished by this War on Drugs. And now with legalization, we have an industry that is dominated by white people making all the profits. We need to make a way for people of color in cannabis, and we need to support each other. As consumers, we need to be educated and read about who exactly we're buying our products from. We need to support people of color who make cannabis products—and also, professionals in the legal cannabis industry can't forget to turn around and open up the door for the people who are right behind us, with partnerships and strategic alliances.

Make Up Your Own Mind

I would ask [young people] to really read and not listen to what just one outlet has to say [about hemp-based foods]—there are so many people out there reporting different things! You can go to the website of the government's National Institutes of Health, which has thousands and thousands of studies on things like CBD. Go read and make up your own mind. Even if it's not for you—which is OK—you'll be able to see why it's important not to keep it from everybody else.

CHAPTER 7
Material for Building a House

Stephen Clarke, Specialist in Hemp-Based Construction

One industry in which hemp could have a huge impact is construction and building, which currently creates 11 percent of worldwide carbon emissions. People have been aware of hemp's potential as a building material since at least the ancient Roman Empire (27 BCE to 476 CE). In northwestern France, for instance, a hardy sixth-century hemp mortar bridge is still standing.

So why aren't hemp houses widely available? Barriers to hemp access began as early as the nineteenth century, when the use of cannabis for its psychoactive purposes began to rise. Laws were enacted worldwide to make cannabis use and possession illegal—a policy change that typically impacted marginalized communities, who are usually the most heavily policed. Regulations surrounding the use of hemp are beginning to change. In the United States, the 2018 Farm Bill legalized hemp cultivation for people and companies with a special permit. China and France are currently the world's largest producers of hemp. Romania, Colombia, and Ecuador also grow lots of the stuff. But in countries such as Mexico, growing hemp continues to be tightly restricted for much of the general population. A 2021 ruling by Mexico's Supreme Court gave one company legal permission to cultivate

The bridge that crosses the Sarthe river in Saint-Céneri-le-Gérei, France, was built by the Merovingians around 500 CE. The secret to the bridge's longevity is its hemp mortar. Typical mortar cracks and chips as it expands and contracts due to fluctuations in temperature and moisture conditions. Hemp mortar is more pliable, allowing it to expand and contract without breaking.

and process hemp. Some hope the federal health ministry will soon give the same right to all Mexicans.

Stephen Clarke is the founder of Mexican sustainable architecture company Heavengrown. He advocates for new laws that would allow everyone to take advantage of hemp's possibilities. Heavengrown teaches people how to make homes from sustainable materials including hempcrete, a mix of hemp, the mineral lime, and water. Hempcrete is a lightweight, pest- and mold-resistant substance that can be molded into blocks or fill in a house's frame to form walls or insulation. Clarke is passionate when it comes to the material's importance in Mexico. In a country where quality building supplies are often hard to come by, and governmental resources are often insufficient to help communities leveled by earthquakes and other natural disasters, spreading knowledge of hemp architecture is equivalent to community-based revolution.

Planting Your Own Home

Hempcrete is a hemp mix that is primarily made from cañamiza, the woodlike filament of the hemp plant. We mix it with lime and water, and it creates a cement-like material. It's a very simple material that allows you to plant your own home. We think that here in Mexico, it is the future.

Hempcrete is made from hemp shives, or cañamiza, a woody waste product from the process of manufacturing hemp fibers.

[In Mexico,] it's legal to build [with hempcrete], and it's legal to import the material, but not to cultivate your own hemp. You have to apply for a special permission. We are supporting a new law that would make hemp cultivation accessible to everyone. We want it to be simple: You take your seeds, plant your hemp, and use it to make your home, paper, batteries—whatever it is you're looking to use it to build.

There are many benefits [of using hempcrete to build a home]. The principal one is thermal. Hemp is a good insulator [you need less energy to keep a hemp-based house warm or cool], flame-resistant, earthquake-resistant. That last part is important in Mexico because there are a large number of earthquakes here. What we have here is a method of planting your own home in a way that yields many benefits. Hempcrete is noble, simple, and it can be made accessible to the entire planet. And it absorbs carbon dioxide, which helps to combat global warming.

Carbon Negative

We're talking about a structure made from a plant that continues absorbing carbon from the atmosphere and, using the photosynthesis process, returns that carbon to the earth. Carbon negative means that every time we plant and build a house, we take more carbon dioxide out of the atmosphere than we put into it. In the construction industry, that's practically impossible, because most building methods create a lot of pollution.

Hemp Keeps Absorbing Carbon Even after a House Is Built

Once we build the house, a settling process takes place in which the lime that we use in the hempcrete mix tries to petrify again. In so doing, the lime pulls more CO_2 from the atmosphere and will continue to do so after the house is built.

These are actually old techniques. Hempcrete is nothing new. It's simply what we've learned from our ancestors, incorporated with modern-day technology.

Local Materials

[Our hempcrete team has] completed about twenty constructions in Mexico. The first project we completed was a home built using traditional Mayan techniques because we wanted to see how hempcrete worked in the weather conditions of the jungle. The problem was that hempcrete has mainly been used in cold climates. I live in a town in the [southeastern Mexican state of] Yucatán that's named Playa del Carmen, where there is a lot of humidity and high temperatures. We weren't sure how hempcrete was going to work here. But we built a Mayan home, and it worked wonderfully! From there, we built a bamboo-hemp structure in a community named Oztopulco located outside the town of Tepoztlán [in the mountainous region outside of Mexico City]. It covers 200 square meters [2,153 sq. feet], its walls are 6 meters [19.7 feet] high, and it was built entirely by volunteers.

In Tulum, we built the tallest hemp building on the continent. It's four stories, almost 20 meters [65.6 feet] high, and it's made with natural materials. We used different kinds of wood that are native to the region, and bamboo. The only material we had to import was the hemp, due to the current legal situation. It's illogical: if we decide to build these buildings using only local Mexican industries, we become criminals! Hemp is a varietal of cannabis that is not psychoactive. And the question is, If it's not psychoactive, why is it so strictly regulated?

Rebuilding after Oaxaca's 2017 Earthquakes

The truth is, it was a very intense experience. We arrived in the southern part of the state, very close to the town of Salina Cruz, Ixtepec. The airport had been so damaged in the earthquake that our plane had to land at the military airport. As we were landing, we could see how the earth had split and swallowed up entire houses. I had never seen anything so horrible. People were very afraid, even days after the quake. They had received very little governmental assistance, it was very chaotic, and many people were homeless.

But there was also a beautiful part of the experience. So many people had come to help. We built three houses in a week in Ixtepec: an adobe house, a house made out of coconuts, and another that we made out of hemp. We donated the homes to people who had lost theirs in the earthquake. It's crazy, because to this day— four years later—there are people who have yet to receive any kind of governmental relief in that area. That's why it's imperative that instead of waiting on the system, we find our own solutions to these issues.

Hemp for Everyone!

We can be what we have always been: grand Toltecs, grand Mayans, grand Mexicas, grand Purepechas, grand Chichimecas. We are a people of so much learning. And yes, the challenges are huge, but at times, challenges are necessary. After that earthquake, the ugliest things were happening, but the human collaboration that resulted was the most beautiful I've seen. It gave me goose bumps, made me think "*This* is Mexico!" And it's in that spirit that we say, "Let's make houses for everyone! Hemp for everyone!"

Big Challenges

We just began to work with coconuts, because hemp is so difficult to import and to get permission to plant. But on the coasts of [the Mexican state of] Guerrero, on the Pacific, there's coconuts everywhere! It's a shame, because cannabis prohibition has led to the disappearance of many hemp varietals. Nowadays, it's quite difficult to find good hemp to grow in Mexico because our weather conditions cause European hemp to flower too quickly. For hempcrete, we don't use hemp flowers; we use its stalks, so we need those stalks to take their time to grow. Hemp can grow to resemble bamboo forests—the fields look nothing like those of the marijuana that we smoke. One of the big challenges that Mexico has is to find varietals that grow well here.

There are so many ways that humans use hemp—for homes, food, energy. These things are—not basic, or simple, those are not good descriptions—they are *primordial* for humans. But until we have better legislation and varietals that are better adapted to our climate, Latin American countries, "third-world" countries, will not be able to take advantage of hemp's many benefits. We're pretty sure that no one has planted hemp in Mexico on a large scale in the last century. We're trying to get back to that, and the impact on the population here is going to be enormous.

Compostable Batteries

We're working on a hemp battery that will replace lithium batteries. You will be able to compost the batteries when you're done using them, they last twenty years, and can be charged rapidly. They're made with a new hemp-based material that is similar to graphene. This is important because all the batteries that we currently use are toxic, because they're made of lithium. Plus, eventually the world's lithium supplies are going to run out. Graphene can also be used to make semiconductors, cell phone screens, even things like water filters.

I Wanted to Change the World

I've lived my whole life in Mexico, but half of my family came from the Caribbean. The way in which I was taught about the plant was very distinct. For us, it is something very sacred. My professional formation is in electronic and computational systems engineering, which made me very stressed out about how the world was going to end up—2000, the Y2K crisis [a worldwide panic that occurred when computer engineers weren't sure how systems would handle the date switching to the new century], all that.

Twenty years ago, I began to look for solutions. I entered a contest in which you had to build a completely solar-powered house. But even though we had all this solar panel technology, the house we built was losing energy through its walls. Mexico has terrible construction materials, so I started to research and found out that one of the best materials to make houses from was hempcrete. Everything just came together. Now I am convinced that the cannabis plant can give us everything we need. I started investigating the uses of hemp that could benefit Mexico, bringing available techniques over here. I've also been in Colombia and Uruguay, and I'm trying to go to as many countries as possible to spread this knowledge. Twenty years ago, I wanted to change the world, and I didn't know how. Today I know exactly what the solutions are and how to do it. And not just with hemp—with coconuts and with bamboo.

What Happened with Tobacco

You have to be careful with the big companies, the big pharmaceutical brands. A lot of people are jumping on board with cannabis because they heard they could make a lot of money off of it. We need to learn from what happened with tobacco, which is one of the most sacred plants in the world. Many Indigenous communities used it in ceremonies. But nowadays, Indigenous people no longer plant tobacco. Today, Philip Morris plants it and puts in all kinds of toxic agrochemicals, to the point where the world thinks of tobacco as something terrible! That could happen to cannabis if we don't take care of it. We're looking to share this seed with the Mexican people, to share the knowledge of how you plant hemp and how it is harvested. Because in Mexico, we have all the right conditions: we have water, we have land, and we have people who need what hemp can provide.

CHAPTER 8
Indigenous Empowerment

Mary Jane Oatman, Editor of *Tribal Hemp and Cannabis Magazine*

More than five thousand groups of Indigenous peoples live around the world. Each one has its own unique history, modern-day community structure, and relationship with cannabis. Some communities make a lot of money from their local marijuana industries, which they self-regulate. Others have been raided by law enforcement for working with weed in a way that runs afoul of the laws of settler-run states or federal colonialist governments. Some communities' leaders have decided that they want nothing to do with cannabis!

But particularly on the American continents, many Indigenous people are working to reclaim their tribes' cannabis stories to learn more about the plant and how it has coexisted with their people. A lot of them question the long-held assumption that cannabis first arrived in the Western Hemisphere with European settlers. Historic documents tell of Indigenous people who had relationships with cannabis that predate the arrival of colonists. Some hypotheses suggest that Indigenous traders could have brought cannabis seeds back from Asia via Pacific Ocean trading routes.

Today, many Indigenous communities see cannabis as an issue related to sovereignty, or their right to self-govern, even if they are geographically located within the jurisdiction of a colonizer government. Recognition of sovereignty rights varies by region, and even by community or nation, because in many places around the world, Indigenous groups have negotiated individual treaties with governments. Sovereignty rights are under constant attack. In 2022 the United States Supreme Court undermined community-based reservation policing when it decided that state governments could prosecute people for alleged crimes committed on reservations.

When sovereignty is recognized, cannabis businesses in Indigenous communities can generate much-needed financial resources and offer products that might not be available in state-run dispensaries.

Making sure Indigenous people profit from marijuana becomes even more important when you consider how they have been impacted by the racially biased War on Drugs. One pre-legalization study in Canada showed that Indigenous people were arrested on cannabis-related charges up to *nine times* more than white people. Drug policing that oppresses Indigenous peoples takes place around the world. The New Zealand government

The Iipay Nation of Santa Ysabel, California, constructed these cannabis greenhouses to support their dispensary.

has published similar findings about the Maori population being arrested and convicted for cannabis crimes at disproportionate rates. Such injustice led New Zealand to give the first license to start a medicinal marijuana business to a Maori-led company. In Oaxaca, Mexico—a country in which Indigenous people have long been caught in the crossfire between drug-selling narcos and Drug War–driven law enforcement—the state government issued twenty-six Indigenous communities licenses to cultivate medicinal cannabis, in a restorative justice–motivated attempt to redistribute profits made from the plant.

A descendant of Chief Looking Glass of the Nez Perce Tribe of the Columbia River Plateau and of the Delaware Tribe, Mary Jane Oatman is an expert on the past, present, and future of First Nations and weed. She has made it her mission to shed light on Indigenous cannabis stories to promote sovereignty rights. She also fights stigmas associated with the plant that prevent Indigenous people from accessing cannabis's many health benefits. Oatman is a staunch promoter of the many Indigenous people who are experts in the kind of regenerative agriculture that the legal cannabis industry needs to employ if it doesn't want to further pollute our planet. She is far from the first Indigenous person to raise their voice on the subject. John Trudell, a member of the Santee Sioux Nation and former American Indian Movement chairperson, often spoke of the powerful role the plant had played in the history of such communities, and he even cofounded a hemp advocacy organization with country musician Willie Nelson.

In 2020 Oatman founded *Tribal Hemp and Cannabis Magazine*, a free print publication (also available online) that provides basic information on cannabis's therapeutic benefits. Here's a not-so-fun fact: the Nez Perce Reservation, where Oatman lives, is in the land known as Idaho, making her the only interviewee in this book who lives in a place where both medicinal and recreational cannabis remain completely illegal. That hasn't stopped *THC Magazine* from profiling Indigenous people who are making waves in the world of weed—and Oatman's grandmother, cannabis cultivator and advocate Alice "Jeanie" Warden, was the magazine's first cover model!

MARY JANE OATMAN

Since I Was in Utero

My parents have both been cannabis users for as long as I can remember. My mother used cannabis to help her through the early stages of her pregnancy with all six of her children, during a time frame when that was really frowned upon. So when I get asked the question, "How long have you been using cannabis?" I say, since I was in utero, since I was in my mother's womb.

I also remember being at the raid on my family's property, when my grandmother and grandfather both went to federal prison for growing marijuana. The shame and the stigma that came after that was really difficult to manage. Especially when I was an elementary school student sitting in the all-school D.A.R.E. assemblies. In the reservation school system in Idaho, everybody knows everybody's business. It never failed— they would come in with McGruff the Crime Dog, and all of the kids' energy and eyeballs in the room shifted over towards all of the little

THC Magazine's first issue featured Alice "Jeanie" Warden, Mary Jane Oatman's grandmother, and documented the family's farming roots in southwestern Idaho.

Oatman-Warden [my maternal grandmother's last name] kids in the assemblies.

But I had a considerable amount of education at home about benefits, about our people's connection with the plant and sacrament. [We learned] that we've always been a smoking people, since before white men ever came to our homelands.

My People Knew That Plants Taught Lessons

The reclamation of all Indigenous peoples' stories as they pertain to cannabis is really in its infancy. There are a lot of communities that have a very robust connection to plant history in a more general sense, but when it comes to their history with cannabis—that can be a little bit more unknown. That's where it's important to take it upon ourselves to dig into the archaeological records, to look into some of the journals of the early settlers that came to our homelands. Western literature from as early as 1829 does document that, specifically in the Nez Perce homelands, we have had a smoking relationship with a green plant that was very different from the white man's tobacco. But there are 574 federally recognized tribes in the United States, and every tribal story is so different and unique.

I know that cannabis did exist here [before settlers came]. Some of the records of the first contact with settlers on the East Coast note that [Indigenous communities used] "hemp cordage," and that we already had a very intimate relationship with hemp as a textile. My people in the Pacific Northwest have been traveling by canoe for thousands of years, and they knew that plants taught lessons. They were always looking for different teaching plants. The Western story is that [settlers] brought these things to us, helped us learn about these things. But the counternarrative to that is that we already have been working and trading in this global community prior to 1492, when Columbus "sailed the ocean blue" and created the "New World."

Indigenous sovereignty is what we were born into. It's every-thing that makes us who we are, our living, vibrant, thriving cultures as Indigenous people. What I see now is that our Indigenous people are taking a step back and seeing a new way to build an economy of bartering and trading that existed during the precolonial times. This cannabis medicine has endured even when it was criminalized, and a lot of that is because our Indigenous community have always talked about the smoke sacrament. John Trudell was a huge ambassador of cannabis as medicine. It is a part of our DNA. That is something that has been instilled in me from a very young age: that I'm connected and related to all of the beings around me, to the water and the fire, and to the plants.

Grandma Was My Inspiration

I love magazines. I grew up flipping through *National Geographic.* I loved looking at its pictures; they really inspired me to embrace photography. And so, as cannabis legalization in Washington began, and I was doing little tours in different cannabis dispensaries, I noticed some of the cannabis publications that were popping up. I thought, "Well, these are really cool," but I flipped through them, and none of them had any tribal stories. I got the idea for the magazine in the fall of 2019. I was working in construction as a traffic control flagger on a very slow project in the middle of nowhere, basically just making sure that nobody drove into a big hole. I was reading everything that I could, voraciously. And I read through this cannabis magazine and thought, "You know what? I bet that some of these advertisers would want to advertise in a tribal magazine." I took sixteen pieces of paper, folded them in half, and started sketching.

On the front cover of my mock-up, I drew a picture of a smiley face, and I said, "That's Grandma. I want Grandma to be on the cover of the first issue of *THC Magazine.*" She was my inspiration.

I didn't know anybody else in my world who had gone to federal prison for growing marijuana and then came home and was still so much in love with the plant and continued to be an ambassador for its medicine, even into her elderhood.

I didn't have any money to start it up—selling ads for a ghost magazine was such a challenge! But I was able to get one of the tribes, the Puyallup tribe in Washington State that operates Remedy dispensary. They threw down! They saw the vision. Since then, it's grown. We chose print publication for *THC Magazine* because with print, we could get this magazine into the hands of our elders as well as our young people, so that they could see that there's pathways towards workforce development, or that there's many ways to consume cannabis besides smoking. It's all about education, because that's what is really needed to help eliminate the fear, for people to see that this is a choice in healing. Oftentimes, because of the way that politics work in tribal communities, our elders have a lot of decision-making power. If they say no [to cannabis], that means that that economic development cannot happen. That's happening still, to this day, because of the lack of information on cannabis.

I've Really Built My Dream Job

When I published the very first issue in February of 2020, we went big. I told my mom and my grandma, I said, "Pack your bags, we're going to Washington, DC, for the launch of *THC Magazine*." And they thought that I was crazy. "What are you talking about?"

I said, "There's a gathering for the tribes of the National Congress of American Indians." We put copies of the magazine in our carry-on bags; we were weighing our bags. We went out with as many magazines as we could! On that first trip, we brought two thousand magazines to Washington, DC. The word started spreading, and soon we were driving *THC Magazine* all over the country. We've just been buckshotting it across the nation so that we could get it out there. We would not have been able to do it without our supporters. Everything that we distribute is free, and there's a lot of heart that goes into each issue. I just feel blessed. I've really built my dream job, and I see it doing nothing but growing.

I Am No Longer Waiting for Permission

The magazine within my own community has been nothing but a healthy conversation starter. It has allowed families to talk about [cannabis] being controversial, to talk about it being healing, to talk about it being possible in Idaho at some point in the future. As an Indigenous woman who walks amongst my homelands, I am no longer waiting for permission from anybody, even from within my own community, to heal myself. That's, I think, probably the biggest fallacy right now, is this whole legal-illegal thing. We know it's good; we know that it's right. And so, I'm not waiting for any settler politician to tell me or give me permission [to work with cannabis]. I feel like the way that I embrace my work with cannabis allows other people to also give themselves permission.

Our young people know more than we do. Our young people understand that Mother Earth makes plants, cannabis is a plant, and plants can be medicine. I want them to know that there is a whole world of learning that we have to do from this plant as we move forward. That doesn't mean smoking it, that doesn't even necessarily mean having to farm with it. We are going to need doctors that are well-trained in cannabis medicine, lawyers that understand legal and political policy changes from a fresh point of view and not from the biased War on Drugs point of view. And we're going to need our young people really looking at shifting the environmental ways that we interact with agriculture. With that being said, I would love to know: What are [young people's] big-picture ideas? How do we implement that? Because they're going to inherit these systems that we built for them.

CHAPTER 9
Fashion
Andrés Rivera, Founder of Hemp Boot Company

Maybe by this point, you are getting the idea that hemp can play a rainbow of roles in a sustainable society. Andrés Rivera has certainly done his part to make sure that cannabis you can wear is on the rise in his hometown of Medellín, Colombia. In 2010 Rivera started his hemp-focused footwear company, Todos Hacemos Cultura, whose name means "We all make culture" in Spanish. He and customers refer to the company by its initials, which it not-so-coincidentally shares with the most famous psychoactive component in cannabis: THC.

In the company's early days, when Colombia's cannabis culture was still underground, THC's name was code for its close-knit community of cannabis-loving customers. That secretiveness was kind of necessary: marijuana users were subject to harsh societal stigma, perhaps because the violent civil war between the Colombian government and the Revolutionary Armed Forces of Colombia (FARC for its initials in Spanish) has been funded in part by profits from the illegal drug industry since its start in 1964. That history has left some of Colombia's population with a hard-to-shake mental association between criminal activity and cannabis—even for plants that have been grown by cultivators that have little to do with organized criminal associations. But Colombia passed its first laws legalizing medicinal cannabis in 2016 and has set in motion important conversations around how drug prohibition has damaged the country. It's becoming easier to envision a future conflict-free weed industry led by independent growers—especially when one looks at THC's workshop and showroom, which occupy a mural-covered third floor of a building in Medellín. The company is known for its colorful takes on hip-hop footwear staples, from tea-green work boots to maroon high-top sneakers built with sturdy, durable cannabis fibers.

Just like many other uses of hemp, the plant's potential as clothing is not new. It was the first documented material humans used to make their outfits, dating back to the Neolithic era (which ended around 4500 BCE) in China. The cannabis plant's strong fibers often grow longer than 6 feet (1.8 m). Hemp matures much faster than wood, doesn't require harmful pesticides, won't rob the soil of nutrients, and provides protection from erosion with its long roots. Hemp absorbs carbon dioxide from the atmosphere—more than twice as much as trees—and needs half the water and area of cotton. This is a big deal in a world where fast fashion has become one of the most serious sources of global pollution! For a

THC produces shoes in a variety of styles for men, women, and children.

long time, hemp was the go-to not only for making clothes but all manner of textile products, from ship sails to Betsy Ross's first US flag. As clothing, hemp fiber can be used to create a flame-resistant material that stands up to heavy wear and tear; is naturally antibacterial, breathable, and warm; and even blocks UV rays.

You'd think we'd all have closets full of hemp looks. But we don't, and by now, you probably know why: cannabis prohibition. Even though it can't get you high, industrial hemp still comes from the same plant species as smokable reefer. As a result, its cultivation and processing have been subject to tight regulations in many places around the world. (China is a big exception. Marijuana prohibition never led that country to shut down its hemp industry, and as a result, China supplies much of the world with it.) Also, since hemp agriculture has been banned in so many places for so long, the special machinery used to process its freakishly strong fibers can be wildly expensive and hard to come by. Lingering restrictions around the world make it impossible to utilize hemp to its full potential.

These hurdles haven't stopped passionate hempsters from searching for workarounds to their hemp sourcing needs. Years ago, Rivera told me, Todos Hacemos Cultura managed to locate a roundabout but reliable supply chain to get the hemp canvas they use to make their boots' upper sections.

ANDRÉS RIVERA

The DNA of Our Cannabis Community

We chose hemp [for our products] because it is the DNA of our cannabis community here in Medellín, Colombia. We saw that cannabis is extremely versatile and is very relevant for our public, whether they are recreational or medicinal consumers, or if they love to grow cannabis or move in the cannabis world in another sense. Hemp has antifungal properties and is good for our environment due to its durability. As a fiber it's a little rough, rustic, with properties that make it pleasant to the touch.

My mother has been a shoemaker her whole life, and through her work, I saw an opportunity for myself in which I could earn income and at the same time satisfy my artistic side. I like footwear because it's a basic element in a scene that I very much appreciate and form part of, which is Medellín's hip-hop community. Clothing and footwear are foundational parts of hip-hop. They give it its aesthetic, identity—really, its style.

It Was a Bit of a Surprise for My Mother

[My mother] has always been very happy that I have chosen to enter her profession, her legacy. But we initially started making our boots out of other materials while we looked for a good source of hemp. [Back then we focused on] leather, synthetic fibers, and other kinds of environmentally friendly fibers. The shoes always had a cannabis theme: leaf prints and images of molecules with our brand name. We didn't start working with hemp until about six or seven years ago. We got our first hemp fiber from our friend Stephen Clarke [see chapter 7], who had been around the world and who was able to get us a delivery of a few meters of hemp canvas. With that, we made the first hemp boots. For me, it was a pleasure as a designer and creator to finally be able to touch the material and make these pieces.

My mother's reaction when she figured out that THC meant something in addition to Todos Hacemos Cultura, that it also referred to tetrahydrocannabinol, and that the brand was focused on personalities from the cannabis world . . . well, it was a bit of a surprise for her! But today, she's helping me with the brand, and she's changed her thinking about marijuana. It's such a versatile plant and has so many uses beyond recreational consumption, getting stoned on the street corner, which I think is how she was perceiving it at the time. Now she talks about the brand with real ownership and pride. Like, "Yes, we make boots with hemp!" She is still learning, but she's definitely getting used to the subject.

Sourcing Materials

The hemp [canvas, for the boots' upper portion] has to be shipped in from outside of Colombia. In Latin America, there's still no company dedicated to the manufacturing of hemp canvas. We currently bring that material in from the United States, from a source in Colorado. I believe that in turn, they source the raw hemp from China. It's all very outsourced, with so many parts of the process that, well, we hope that at some point it's simplified, for many reasons.

Barriers to Production

The shipping process makes the final product much less sustainable. It's too bad because planting hemp helps a lot with the reduction of soil erosion, and its cultivation does not require as many chemicals as other crops. But at the same time, we can't grow hemp here because we don't have permission from the government. Right now, the regulation[s] around licenses for growing hemp are relatively new and somewhat strict.

Other [challenges] include the professional knowledge needed, plus the money and machinery. I've spoken with various colleagues who have tried to do manufacturing here, but they say that the machinery is too costly. Hemp is a rough material compared with cotton, linen, or other natural fibers. It requires a different kind of machinery and sewing needle to process, in addition to the knowledge needed to operate that machinery, which is another barrier.

How We Make It Happen

We have boots whose exteriors are 100 percent hemp. Then we have other models that have parts made from leather and from cannabis, and others made from a blend of synthetic fibers and hemp. For about a year, we've been making boots whose soles are made from cannabis that is grown here in the city by cultivator friends for whom the hemp stalk—which is where fiber comes from—is usually a waste product. They're more interested in the plant's flower. But we can recycle the stalk, put it through a drying process, mash it up, and mix it with a natural rubber. We then put this mix in a mold to form the sole. It's very cool that we can have a shoe whose exterior is made 100 percent from hemp, from the sole to its upper—the interiors are made with cotton or recycled polyester. We're working to make our workshop 100 percent hemp-focused. But we need to be able to buy the necessary hemp.

Right now we have five permanent collaborators. My mother leads the production side, which includes manufacturing and sewing, and two other people work with her. One of them is Leidy, who is my partner, and who helps me on the administrative side. There's Santiago, who is the runner. He takes care of purchasing and other things. We have two other coworkers, one who is in charge of cutting pieces and various other steps, and the other who is in charge of gluing the soles. So we're six, if you count me. Sometimes during seasons with high demand, we hire more people and there's eight to ten of us.

We have our own store attached to our workshop in Medellín's Aranjuez neighborhood. There are also other multi-brand stores that buy one or two designs from us to complement their clothing lines. Sometimes to round out one of our collections, we will do collaborations with friends who specialize in making hats, fanny packs, or other kinds of bags.

Five Major Brands That Played the Hemp Card

It was high time for these companies and designers to start exploring the more environmentally sustainable options of hemp clothes and footwear.

Nike is a big hemp fan—the athletic brand has dropped multiple versions of its iconic Air Force 1 shoes made with cannabis fiber, in addition to other wearables. But it's the label's canna collabs with streetwear legend **Stüssy** that have gotten hypebeasts most excited. In 2022 the two companies linked up for a bone-colored take on the beloved Air Force 1 Mids called the Fossil. With hemp uppers and recycled rubber soles, the kicks make hemp look haute.

Fashion designer **Donatella Versace** once sent a luminous, open-back hemp-silk gown down a runway in support of Earth Pledge, an environmental nonprofit. The show, which kicked off New York Fashion Week 2008, featured stunning

A model in hemp walks the runway at the Earth Pledge FutureFashion show in 2008.

designs made from earth-friendly fabrics, including a hemp pantsuit developed by Calvin Klein designer Francisco Costa.

Levi's was one of the first big brands to invest in a large-scale release of hemp clothes and has been gradually working more of the fabric into its offerings, starting in 2019 with WellThread and Outerknown, clothing lines that included hemp-blend slim-fit jeans and western-style shirts. The brand has made a big deal out of its "cottonized hemp." It processes it to be as soft as its standard offerings, and regularly drops wearables with up to 50 percent hemp origin.

California activewear company **Patagonia** has been working with hemp blends since 1997. Today you can cop hemp canvas vests and overalls, tank tops, and drawstring shorts from the company, which announced it would start looking to source its hemp fiber from the United States when the 2018 US Farm Bill legalized its production.

One of the United States' most iconic designers dropped a bombshell when he revealed that he'd quietly been using hemp as a clothing material for a decade. In 1995 **Ralph Lauren** told the press that he'd debuted cannabis wearables in his 1985 safari collection and raved about hemp's rugged look. In 2022 Lauren released several more sustainable, durable garments made from a hybrid hemp-cotton material called clarus.

Our Customers

They have some environmental consciousness; they love the cannabis plant—many of them work with the plant in some way. They like hip-hop and reggae music, although their musical tastes can vary. They support independent businesses and value art. They're a little nonconformist. They have an independent vision, and they're a little rebellious, but at the same time, they're fun and have an interest in creating things in community.

Hemp for Life Is the Recipe

[People's attitudes on cannabis are] changing a lot. And yes, people's interest in hemp fiber is growing. Some of them because it simply draws their attention, or because it sounds trendy. But the desire to have something made out of hemp is growing. There's a phrase in which I find a lot of inspiration: "Hemp for life is the recipe." ["Cáñamo para la vida es la receta."] It's a phrase that we use as a motto for the store. This is the number one plant that could someday save this planet. It can give us food, clothing, medicine. It can give us so much.

CHAPTER 10
Narco Ballads . . . and a Religious Icon
Ely Quintero, Corridos Singer

I think learning about the Mexican drug economy should be required in United States schools. It mainly exists to supply drug users in its neighbor to the north! On the flip side, the production of cannabis has also provided employment for a hell of a lot of people in Mexico, many of whom you couldn't very accurately call narcos. Many of these individuals are small-scale farmers living in sparsely populated sierras of states such as Guerrero, Oaxaca, Michoacán, Durango, and Sinaloa, with few employment alternatives. Other people who hold low-level positions in the drug trade live in less rural areas through which illegal substances are trafficked. Statistics of how many Mexicans are employed by the illegal economy are hard to come by, due to the secrecy of organized crime operations. But the economic and cultural presence of the drug trade, including the trafficking of cannabis, has become a part of life in many areas.

Culiacán, the capital of Sinaloa, is the site of a chapel built in honor of the long-gone, potentially mythic robber baron Jesús Malverde, who has become a kind of folk saint. He is not recognized by the Catholic Church, but many refer to him as the angel of the poor. Malverde's followers have decorated the chapel's walls with homemade plaques honoring him. Many of

A bust of folk saint Jesús Malverde is illuminated by candles at the Culiacán chapel that honors him.

these tributes are adorned with automatic weapons and, yes, marijuana leaves.

Singer Ely Quintero, who lives in Culiacán, knows all about cannabis's complex role in her community. She was born in the small town of Badiraguato, also the birthplace of Joaquin "El Chapo" Guzmán, one of the most notorious drug traffickers in the world, a former leader of the powerful organized crime group the Sinaloa Cartel, and the son of a humble local agricultural family. When she was beginning her musical career, Quintero moved to the United States to perform grupera music. You might know the rock-inspired mega-genre from its superstar Selena Quintanilla, or Selena, as her fans more often refer to her.

Quintero later began singing corridos, ballads that emerged in the nineteenth century. Since the Mexican Revolution (1910–1920), corridos have told tales of larger-than-life heroes and antiheroes. The 1970s saw the rise in popularity of narcocorridos, odes to the Mexico crime bosses who run the country's shadow economy. In the twenty-first century, artists began producing corridos verdes (green corridos), whose smoky song lyrics often referred to the consumption of cannabis. This partial shift in focus from people who trafficked weed to those who smoked it coincided with the legalization of recreational marijuana in California, where many of these artists were based.

Given the communities in which Quintero was raised, it's no surprise that her songs often tell stories of the illegal drug trade, such as one ballad in which her police-pursued narrator is the romantic partner of a Sinaloa Cartel boss. Other tracks tell of the people employed at drug packing facilities—the ones boxing up cannabis and other substances to be shipped north to sell to gringos. But "Quiero Andar al 420" [roughly translated "I Want to Be High"], perhaps Quintero's most famous track, is the epitome of a corrido verde. For Quintero, her music is an opportunity to tell stories about the place she grew up, narratives that defy the official line that all those who are involved in the vast drug economy—producers and consumers alike—are degenerates.

In our interview, Quintero explained what cannabis means in Sinaloa, a place where outlaws can be considered community leaders—and sometimes saints.

Ely Quintero's music pays homage to the musical and economic history of Culiacán.

Narco Ballads ... and a Religious Icon

ELY QUINTERO

What Makes Sinaloa Special

[Sinaloa has a unique relationship with the cannabis plant] because we grow it here with very organic techniques in the sierra—up in the hills. [Farmers] have to plant in parts of the mountains that aren't visible to soldiers, to the government. There are no water lines up there, and people put a lot of effort into running hoses that can connect a cannabis-growing operation to a well, often many kilometers away. I don't know if other states grow cannabis like this. But here in Sinaloa, people do, and the land receives it well. I think that's what makes it special.

When I was a few months away from turning five years old, I learned that [cannabis] was a topic of discussion in our community, in the whole ranching area. Why? Because it provides employment. You start to see the plant as something normal, as a source of jobs. It was free from the stigma that this noble plant suffers from in other parts of society. Every once in a while, I'd be walking next to the arroyo [stream] and I'd see a plant growing. That was normal too. No stigma! But people from my hometown rarely consumed the marijuana themselves. It was just their livelihood.

The Government Would Send Helicopters

I remember how, all of a sudden, there would be a commotion in our town because a rumor would start [that] the soldiers were coming [to raid the marijuana fields]. The people in Badiraguato would send someone—a little boy or a teenager—up the mountain so that he could see if they were coming. Sometimes, women would go to look for their husbands to warn them to leave the marijuana fields. Because the government would send helicopters, that kind of thing.

Create and Not Destroy

[The Mexican government] has taken it upon itself to run a very destructive campaign. They [present] cannabis as something destructive. The way I see it, it's a campaign based on other interests. Because when something is prohibited, it doesn't just generate morbid interest. It also generates a lot of money for the people who are still able to [illegally] bring it from one place to another. So [in the government's response to cannabis], I see an economic interest in making sure it's heavily stigmatized. I think what they *should* do is try to create a new kind of consciousness about the drug. People should know that the plant can be used to create and not destroy. I know a lot of people who are very, very creative—people who work in music, in painting, in sculpture, and in other areas as well—who use cannabis as a stimulus to wake up their creative engines, to make beautiful, impressive projects.

I think that it's due to sensationalism that many people judge marijuana so much. They see it as the worst in the world, but it's because of a lack of understanding. I don't see it in that way. I see it as a way for people to make a living.

The Patron Saint

Jesús Malverde is the patron saint of the narcos. He is a very mystic figure, who likely lived around 150 years ago. Malverde holds a lot of significance in terms of faith, not only for the narcos but for other people, people who are desperate, who find themselves in complicated situations. They go to Malverde and ask him for a miracle. I've spoken with people who tell me that he delivered when they asked.

For the narcos, this faith is something in which they can take refuge, something in which they can deposit their concerns over their work. And who better for that than a person with whom they identify? Malverde was from Sinaloa, and he was a bandit. He robbed in the name of God in order to give to the poor. He had a cause and a purpose. And I think that the narcos from here, they have a cause and a purpose as well. I think that's what makes the link, that magical and grand mysticism of Jesús Malverde with their faith. They even write corridos about him. People wear his medallion, or a hat with Malverde on it. He has a lot of marketing. [His followers honor him with marijuana images] because of their business. If you're a narco, you could be carrying a load of marijuana, on the run from the government. And in that case, you're asking Malverde to protect your marijuana. When they bring him things with marijuana leaves on them, they are a kind of offering. It's like you're identifying what it is you need help protecting. I'm sure it would be the same if all of a sudden tobacco was prohibited. You would see tobacco cigarettes in the Malverde chapel. The marijuana leaf is a spiritual symbol, in this case. It's economic, about protecting one's business interests.

I Have to Make a Song about Marijuana— Maybe Two!

In this world, there are as many people who consume marijuana as there are who consume music. And many of the people who consume marijuana follow the music of Ely Quintero! I really started to get that when I played some concerts in California, where marijuana is more legal. Here in Sinaloa, people have to hide when they smoke marijuana, but in California, it doesn't matter as much. Fans would come up to me and be like, "Viejona! Come on, let's smoke." Then I began to see how corridos about marijuana were beginning to sell. I said, "I have to make a song about marijuana. One—maybe two!" Because it's real!

My Most Famous Song

["Quiero Andar al 420"!] It talks about real things! There's one part where the narrator says that her mom walked in on her smoking . . . that's all real! The lyrics aren't from a single person's story, though. They were various people who I spoke to when I was looking for things to include in the song. People like it. They know I'm not singing any lies. [laughs]

I Respect Cannabis

I've tried it—I had to try it. This is the first time I've said that in public, and I'm saying it to you! I had to see what kind of effects it could have on my music. Before I wrote ["Quiero Andar al 420"]. I had to know.

[I'm not a regular consumer,] but I respect cannabis. Everyone has their own ways of doing things, of relaxing, of hanging out. I have my own ways. And I grew up in a world where they plant it and sell it, but they don't consume it. So I have that programming in me, somehow.

Hard Workers, Humble People

Someone has to sing for those who are looked at as the bad guys. They only get judgment, judgment, judgment—and that's not how I see them. I see hard workers, humble people, who if you go to their home will give you everything they own. If it's time to eat, they'll make you food and give you a meal. They'll give you a roof to sleep under; they'll always say "please" and "thank you." I learned my manners with them. The formation of who I am as a person—that was my school, and I know it. It's what I carry with me here, in my mind and my heart.

They're real people, real human beings, and someone has to sing for them. Everything has a good side and a bad side. Marijuana has a good side and a bad side. It's just a question of educating people. If you like weed, that's OK—just use it correctly, that's all. Make something cool while you're stoned. [laughs]

Documenting History

Stories of criminals have always been present in corridos, and there have always been very famous narcos. It's always been like that. You could write a thousand books about this, with a thousand incredibly interesting stories, and they would be bestsellers because it's always been like this. Prohibition causes all of this. Until cannabis is legal—and I don't know for what God-fearing reason the marijuana is not legal. It wouldn't take much, and so much harm has been caused. So much power, so much money.

Use It Responsibly

Young people: Talk to your parents! Talk with them about your worries, about any guilty feelings. You shouldn't feel guilty because [consuming marijuana] is not something bad; it's a blessed plant. But you do need to use it responsibly—and not use it as an escape from your life. When you use it as an escape, that's when you can get lost. Not just in marijuana, in other substances as well. If you don't trust your parents, maybe your older sibling or your aunt who spoils you, your grandmother. Someone who you trust. Cannabis is less harmful than smoking tobacco—*that* I don't recommend to anyone. [laughs]

CHAPTER 11
Stories behind the Reggae Anthems
Firstman, Creator of Rastafari Indigenous Village

F ew places in the world have contributed as much to global cannabis culture as Jamaica. You may know this if you've ever jammed to the anti-prohibition reggae anthems of the island's 1970s Rastafari singing legends Bob Marley and Peter Tosh. But the island nation's history with the drug is much more complex than many reggae fans are aware.

In 2015 the country decriminalized weed, removing criminal punishments for possession of up to 2 ounces (57 g) of the plant. Jamaica became an even more popular destination for tourists to puff their way through its world-famous ganja. This local term for marijuana likely came to Jamaica from early twentieth-century indentured laborers from India. But the drug is also linked to the historical oppression of the Rastafari community. Authorities often used Rastas' drug use as an excuse to persecute their communities and even take away their homes.

These days, some of the world's richest people capitalize on the world's dim understanding of the Jamaican cannabis legacy. The billionaire founder of PayPal and vocal Donald Trump supporter Peter Thiel, for instance, is one major investor. Thiel is not a Rasta, nor has he ever had to deal with the police's violent monitoring of Rastafari communities. But he profits from the legal cannabis brand that bears Bob Marley's name and is sold in California. Anyone planning a cannabis tourism trip in Jamaica, wearing their hair in the Rastas' traditional dreadlocks—or even just singing along to Peter Tosh's iconic 1976 track "Legalize It" in the comfort of their home—would do very well to educate themselves on these past and present inequities.

Playlist: Jamaica's Legalization Anthems

Many Jamaican reggae artists have addressed the inequities of cannabis prohibition in song. Queue these tracks that tackle the issue:

- "Police in Helicopter," John Holt
- "Rebel Music (3 O'Clock Roadblock)," Bob Marley
- "Ooh LaLaLa the Weed Thing," Hempress Sativa
- "Herbman Hustling," Sugar Minott
- "Tired Fi Lick Weed Inna Bush," Jacob Miller
- "Weed Persecution," Buju Banton
- "Legalize It," Peter Tosh

Cannabis consumer Bob Marley is considered one of the pioneers of reggae, as well as a Rastafari icon. He made Jamaican music popular outside of his home country.

To learn about marijuana in Jamaica, you have to start with the Rastafari. The island-born mindset and way of life goes back to the nineteenth century, when the island was a British colony (as it remained until 1962). Under that colonial government, wealthy, non-Black members of society largely ignored or belittled the African heritage of most of Jamaica's inhabitants, many of whose ancestors had been enslaved and brought forcibly from their homelands to the island. Rastas rejected the anti-Black beliefs of the "system" and often lived in communities that valued natural living and respect for all creatures and plants. Cannabis has long been popular among the Rastafari and is used during ceremonial sessions of drumming and chanting inspired by the traditions of the Afro-Jamaican faith Kumina.

As the popularity of the anti-colonial Rasta lifestyle grew, so too did the British-run government's attempts at oppression of the autonomy-seeking Black communities. In 1954 law enforcement officials descended on Pinnacle, a town founded by one of Rastafarianism's most important leaders, Leonard Percival Howell. Authorities arrested over one hundred people and burned more than 3 tons (2.7 t) of the cannabis that the community had been cultivating. The biggest marijuana raid in Jamaican history (at the time) was the start of a series of attacks that led to Pinnacle's permanent destruction four years later. Rastas were displaced again in the 1960s, when a Kingston neighborhood named Back-o-Wall was razed to the ground and replaced with public housing projects. Such persecution made it nearly impossible for Rastas to form sustainable communities—and to easily practice cannabis cultivation. As a result of limited growing options, Rastafari often had to use harmful agricultural chemicals on their plants, contrary to their healthy-living beliefs. Since 2015's decriminalization, Rastas have continued to fight to expand cannabis access in Jamaica, arguing that high registration fees for cultivators and restrictions on the plant's spiritual uses continue to put their community at risk of criminal penalties.

In 2007 Rastafari founded a working community and educational complex in Montego Bay to correct the historical amnesia surrounding their people and traditions. Rastafari Indigenous Village offers tours that explore the Rasta mindset, cultural heritage, and traditional lifestyle. Experts teach tourists about the organic ital diet (from the word *vital*, ital is a plant-based, whole-foods culinary tradition that is foundational to the faith), drumming ceremonies, and the community's interactions with the ganja plant. Village residents grow it alongside fruits and vegetables in on-site permaculture gardens. The project has implications beyond reclaiming the Rastas' historical legacy. Across the world, communities that have legalized cannabis are struggling with what to do with visitors seeking cannabis tourism experiences.

This mural in the Rastafari Indigenous Village was painted by resident artist and woodworker Michael Earl Bodoo. The piece shows a scene from the Jamaica government's history of policing Rastafari cannabis growers. Its presence, along with the information shared by tour guides to the site, teaches visitors of the plant's past and present within the Rasta community.

Rastafari Indigenous Village founder Firstman explained to me how such marijuana tourism can be an important tool for respectful visitors to the island in learning about one of the world's most famous and poorly understood marijuana cultures.

Weed

FIRSTMAN

People Being Free

My family are the strictest Christians you'll ever meet. I was brought up to avoid the Rastafaris. A young friend of mine gave me a Bob Marley cassette when I was about seventeen, at a time in which I hadn't made that connection with the "systems"—it was just an unnatural world for me, personally. I didn't know exactly what was happening, just that I didn't fit in.

[In the Rastafari community, I found] people being free but still productive and creative in their own sense. People who were scrutinizing and asking questions in relation to what we were accepting as daily life. I found that in the Rastafari faith.

Preserve, Protect, Promote

As Rastafari, we are still facing a lot of exploitation to our community and what we stand for, and there is little understanding of the level of atrocities that have gone on with the community of Rastafari in Jamaica. We recognized that the best way to [guard] culture was embedded in the three p's: You must *preserve* it, you must *protect* it, and you must *promote* it. We created this space where we could set a narrative for ourselves and for our children.

Atrocities against Our Community

When I was growing up, I was taught that England is our mother country, and about the uncivilizedness of Africa. The Rastafari community tries to destroy that narrative with the truth of Africa. We declare that the god of the Christian world is not in our image, and instead, we embrace Emperor Haile Selassie [of Ethiopia]. In 1963 [Jamaican prime minister Alexander] Bustamante paid people to bring the community of Rastafari to the authorities, dead or alive. Thousands, hundreds of Rastafari lost their lives. Until recently, there were places in the Caribbean that had what is called the Dread Act, [which] is still on the books. If [a non-Rasta] got into a fight with a Rasta man, and [the Rasta] lost their life, [the non-Rasta] could not go to jail for it. Our children are even discriminated against in school. [In 2020 a Jamaican court ruled that a school was allowed to suspend a five-year-old girl for wearing dreadlocks.] That's in the twenty-first century.

We Interact with Marijuana as an Entity

One of the main roles that ganja plays in this journey of Rastafari is the full recognition that human beings are not the only consciousness. Because the Rastafari does not *use* marijuana. We *interact* with marijuana as an entity, no different from how people have all different types of animals for pets. They recognize these entities as not necessarily a part of the human world, and they respect them accordingly. Similarly, we recognize ganja as a part of the conscious world, one that is much, much older than the actual human world. It gives us information that allows us to scrutinize ourselves, our behavior, our attitudes. This particular relationship has opened—not altered but opened—our minds to a new way of thinking, to a new way of "overstanding" what the human world has created in its fear. It gives us a way to synchronize a bit better with ourselves and with the planet around us.

Visitors in the Village

Once you're interacting at Rastafari Indigenous Village, you're basically interacting with ganja. It is a strong part of our attitude and behavior. Ganja is assisting us to become our own becoming. We share with [visitors] the different ways in which we interact [with ganja], and the impact that it has on ourselves, our family, our thought process, and so on. We don't normally give people the plant to interact with; they have to seek that relationship for themself. But we ourselves are the attitude and behavior of the plant, and that's what we present. Visitors can also go down to our farm when we have [cannabis] plants down there. Here in the village space, we have a kind of permaculture system that allows us to interact with the plant in its natural environment, without using any kind of chemicals—but not just for cannabis, that goes for all the food that we grow.

Post-Decriminalization Tourism

The village started roughly in 2007, and we have always presented the plant within our space. When decriminalization came about in 2015, we were already recognizing our right to interface with the plant. But in the general Rastafari community, we became able to move around with herb a lot freer, with less fear of the system.

[Tourism] has increased a lot [since decriminalization]. Tourists always want to go to a ganja farm, and we have seen them pop up all over the island. Everybody's doing it now, not just Rastafari.

This Plant Can Change the World

The conversation of legacy communities and minority groups is always important to recognize, within any framework. But the mission of Rastafari is for complete legalization. [Ganja] should not be regulated by people, as it is a natural plant of the earth. So the issue is not how human beings should interact with the plant. It's more about whether the plant can be free. Prohibition has created stories [about ganja], and [now that it is decriminalized] everyone is just jumping in on it without the type of reverent relationship that is required. But we are convinced that the plant is the one leading this process—it's not governments and regulations that are doing it. All we try to do is pick up the flow and the direction of the plant's own liberation mission and try our best to follow the path. This plant can change the world, in terms of nutrition. It can change the world in terms of biodegradable materials. It can change the world in terms of clean air. It can change the world in terms of taking poverty-stricken people and putting them into an industry that they can create for themself. There's a lot of aspects of this plant that can fix what we call "the mental disorder of the human family" at this particular time.

[I hope that visitors to the village] would be able to see a perspective of life that is not driven out of fear. That they can find a way to relate to their neighbors, and I'm not talking about their human neighbors—but their planetary neighbors, the plant world, the animal world. That they will find a way to recognize that human beings are not the owners of the planet, but that they are just a part of the planet. We hope that they would see our reverence and develop respect for these types of conversations.

The Plant Requires Responsible Behavior

The plant requires respect. For teenagers, we certainly recommend interaction on different levels [as compared with adults]. A lot of our own children do not smoke. Many youths are looking for a light in the unreal world, and that brings them to many experiments, ganja being one. But if they're not responsible enough, they will bring a very bad name to the plant, because of how they treat it. Prohibition has given the plant a bad reputation. But the fact that [young people] have to hide [to consume cannabis], that is also a way in which the plant will have a bad reputation. We would urge teenagers to try to wait until they get to the age of consent. Not because [ganja consumption] is bad, but because the plant itself requires their protection, it requires responsible behavior. We would really love for them to look into the history of the Rastafari's particular journey with the plant—not to make it more difficult for the plant to liberate itself. These plants, for a lot of Indigenous and traditional communities, are really about the inspiration and light within oneself, defining oneself. It is important that [young people] see that the traditional way of the plant has been a liberator [for] a lot of people.

Part 3

THE FIGHT FOR DRUG WAR JUSTICE

CHAPTER 12
The Reason Why You Went to Prison

Mauro Melgar, Auto Shop Owner and Former Cannabis Prisoner

Mauro Melgar was seventeen years old when he was riding in the car of a friend who forgot to put on the turn signal. Cops pulled them over in front of Mauro's parents' house in Southern California and found weed in the car. His mom and dad are Guatemalan immigrants, and they didn't have the financial means to pay for an expensive lawyer to represent his case. Mauro was sentenced as an adult and forced to spend a year in state prison, sharing a triple-layer bunk bed with thin mattresses with two other inmates.

The United States incarcerates a higher percentage of its residents than nearly any other nation in the world, and Black people and other people of color who sell unlicensed cannabis get arrested and go to jail at much higher rates than their white peers. Of the 1.43 million people who served time in US prisons between 1975 and 2019, about 20 percent had a drug crime recorded as their most dire offense. People are getting rich off of this bloated prison-industrial complex—governments' and private businesses' profitable collaboration in incarceration. It has fueled a dramatic expansion of the US prison population. US taxpayers spend $81 billion on incarcerating people every year, funds that often go to private corporations that provide services to incarcerated individuals who have no choice in the matter. In some cases, those private corporations run the prisons.

Melgar got out of prison over a decade ago. He runs his family's auto glass replacement business. Not everyone is so lucky. Though cannabis was legal in some form in thirty-eight states and Washington, DC, in 2022, many thousands of people are still imprisoned on cannabis charges in the United States. Exact numbers are hard to come by, and the last official count of weed prisoners was for 2004, numbers released by the underfunded government agency that monitors them. Back then, forty thousand people were serving time for cannabis. And that's in a country where sales of legal cannabis are predicted to hit $80 billion by 2030.

To call this unfair is to put it mildly. Compounding the problem is that in many states, weed-related charges on people's criminal records—which can prevent them from getting jobs, qualifying for public housing, or even voting—are often not automatically erased by cannabis legalization. That means people are incarcerated for nonviolent drug "offenses" that aren't considered crimes anymore! Often individuals with cannabis charges must go through time-consuming legal processes and pay expensive lawyer fees to erase their criminal records. Getting a cannabis crime taken off your record (known as expungement) can be so complicated that activists have founded groups such as National Expungement Works to assist people.

Out of all the interviewees in this book, Melgar may provide the best explanation of how cannabis legalization doesn't solve all the inequities incurred by the Drug War. In our interview, he was frank about how being jailed for a plant that people now make big and legal bucks off has forever impacted the trajectory of his life. His testimony shows the urgent need for political changes in drug policy that prioritize human rights over prison industry profits.

MAURO MELGAR

I Didn't Think I Was Doing Anything Bad

I grew up in Inglewood, California, and I first tried cannabis there when I was a teenager. I didn't really fall in love with it right away. Then my dad decided to move the family to Sun Valley. There was a lot of gang violence in Inglewood, but my dad didn't know that gangs are everywhere, in every city.

My favorite thing to do back in those days was to hang out with the friends I had made in school. My hobbies were helping out at my family's auto shop and spending time with my mom and dad. I made the mistake of dropping out of high school, thinking I could make a living selling weed. In Sun Valley, they had better-quality cannabis—different strains and colors. My mind was blown, and it became a part of my everyday life. But I couldn't find people who sold it, so I decided that I wanted to be that person to spread the love, the happiness. I started selling to kids at my high school in Sun Valley. I didn't think I was doing anything bad selling flowers, but the laws of prohibition were against my actions. In those days you were able to make good money off of weed.

A Felony for the Weed and a Misdemeanor for the Gun

[I was arrested] on Labor Day weekend. It was just bad luck. We had been partying all day, and I asked my friend for a ride home. He made a turn and didn't put his blinker on, so we got pulled over. I had just bought two ounces [56 g], and I had them all bagged up in baggies. The cop asked us to roll the window down. He smelled the weed and asked who had it. We had actually gotten pulled over right in front of my family's house, and my parents came out when they saw the cop car's lights. They didn't know what was going on. The cops handcuffed me and took me to jail.

I got caught with the weed and a gun. [I had the gun] for protection—the people in the area, they weren't so friendly. The [police] made a bigger deal over the weed than the gun. They gave me a felony for the weed and a misdemeanor for the gun.

[After I got arrested] I bailed out [paid a fee to wait for sentencing at home instead of in prison]. It was my first offense. I'd never been arrested. The cops arrested me when I was seventeen, but my court date wasn't until after I turned eighteen, so they tried me as an adult. [The prosecuting attorney] offered me a year in the county jail. I thought, you know, because of the gun . . . I've seen other people get caught with guns and they give them multiple years in jail. So when they offered me a year, I jumped on it. Now it's like, times have changed. A year for weed seems like a lot. There's weed shops everywhere.

Freedom Is Awesome

I was in a California state prison, the one by Six Flags. It was a different world, different rules. I really don't recommend going to jail, it's not fun. All your freedom gets taken away; it's not a good place to be. Freedom is awesome.

Some [people] were [there on drug charges,] and some other people were there on different crimes, like domestic violence, grand theft auto, robberies, assault with a deadly weapon. You know, crazy stuff. I was locked up with a bunch of older people. I was barely eighteen. I was very young.

I feel like I traumatized my parents by going to jail. They are old school, and back in their country, cannabis is illegal to this day.

This Is Not a Game

[Getting out of jail] was a blessing. You don't want to be in jail. The food's horrible. You have to shower in front of other people, go to the bathroom in front of other people. It was just very, very bad. Not good. If you mess up on one of the rules, they beat you up. Luckily, I learned very quickly and decided that I wasn't going to get beat up. Just seeing other people get beat up—it was like damn; this is not a game.

I even went to the hole [solitary confinement]. They put me in a little isolated cell by myself. It was very bad. After two weeks in there, I was counting the days. I was banging on the door, saying, "Hey, get me out of here! I don't want to be in here!" It was traumatizing. You come out of jail thinking differently.

After I Got Out

The felony charge affected my life drastically after I got out. I would look up job listings on Craigslist, just to read that people with a felony were not being hired. Do not get me wrong, I could have gotten a job at a fast-food place, but I was not given the opportunity to be hired at other places. I would apply, but I'd get rejected. I wouldn't get called back. I knew I needed to support my pops and his family, but because of me not being [able] to get a good job, we lost our house. It has impacted me a lot, you know?

I kind of just gave up and decided to join my dad's business, which is an auto glass replacement shop. I eventually took it over in 2012, and we're still in business today. I've done a pretty good job at mastering the craft. Now I live in Sun Valley, over my shop.

I feel like incarceration damages people's lives. Luckily, ten years after I got out of prison, I found out about an expungement event that my friend Felicia was throwing. I was able to get my charge expunged.

Things Happen for a Reason

[Prison is] definitely not [an appropriate punishment]. It's just politicians benefiting off of the tax money and revenue that is being created. There should be a different way of handling these cases.

[If I hadn't been arrested,] I don't know, [maybe I'd be] making money, but things happen for a reason. Now I'm trying to get my high school diploma, things that I didn't pay that much importance to back in those days because I was young. I need a few more credits to graduate.

After Legalization

[The government is] not even trying to repair the harm that was done [by cannabis prohibition]. [They] just went along with the plan to make money. After the expungement event, I saw that [the City of Los Angeles] was trying to move rapidly with the cannabis industry and licenses. They were discussing a social equity program that was promised to help those negatively impacted [by the Drug War]. But they were just trying to move along and get the licenses out in a way that didn't really help those of us who were impacted.

You Need to Speak Up

I actually felt like the universe was saying to me, "Hey, they're talking about you. You need to speak up." So, I went to City Hall. The first time, it was like an icebreaker. I didn't know, you know, that these were the people who run the city. That this is where all my tax money goes to. Then the second time, I went prepared. I wrote a little something [about my experience going to jail for cannabis] and I read it out loud and I didn't think that it was going to mean anything. Like, who cares about my life, you know? But I ended my speech, and I turned around, and everybody was clapping for me. It was an eye-opener.

What Do I Want Readers to Know?

Take school seriously. Don't make the mistake of dropping out. You're stronger with education.

CHAPTER 13
Protest

Miguel Fernández, Cultivator and Founding Member of Plantón 420

C annabis activists have used many tactics to fight for access to the plant and against the inequalities associated with cannabis policing. In California, 1990s HIV/AIDS activists noted that the drug seriously alleviated nausea and other symptoms associated with the virus. They raised awareness about the need for medicinal marijuana by opening public but technically illegal stores that catered to people living with HIV and AIDS. In 2014 Alaskan television news reporter Charlo Greene quit her job during a live broadcast, announcing that she'd be dedicating herself to working in cannabis. The attention generated by her bold move helped pass the state's first recreational marijuana legalization laws two months later. From Canada to Argentina, thousands have attended demonstrations such as the Global Marijuana March, aimed at ending prohibition. The rally has been held in over one thousand cities since 1999.

In Mexico, where weed has been grown for generations, passionate people have found many ways to demonstrate their support for legalization. In states such as Oaxaca and Morelos, groups of campesinos have organized for their right to lawfully cultivate the plant. In Mexico City, smack dab in front of the visitor's entrance of the country's Senate building, cannabis activists established a semipermanent, residential protest camp from 2020 to 2023. The site, called Plantón 420, offered a place for people to consume cannabis twenty-four hours a day without fear of police persecution, thanks to the country's right to freedom of expression when one is protesting. It also hosted a tall, bushy marijuana garden where volunteers learned about cannabis cultivation and whose primary purpose was to teach passersby about the true nature of a heavily stigmatized plant.

The word *plantón* (a place where you "plant" something) refers to a protest strategy of occupying public land for extended periods to bring attention to a cause. The method has long been popular among Latin American activists.

Cannabis grows in flowerpots at Plantón 420 in Mexico City. The plants, which are grown openly in front of the country's Senate, were a symbol of resistance for those who seek to legalize cannabis and its derivatives. The protest camp cultivated more than ten thousand plants.

What was it like to put personal safety on the line for the cannabis movement? In 2022, I spoke to one of the protest camp's founding activists and head cultivators, Miguel Fernández, to try to understand what drove the people of the plantón.

MIGUEL FERNÁNDEZ

I Grew Up around the Plants

I come from a family that worked in the transportation of marijuana from Oaxaca to Harlingen, Texas, and across the southern United States. In the 1980s, my dad started paying a quota of his income [to organized crime groups] to be able to transport marijuana from independent cultivators in Oaxaca to the United States as an independent contractor. Back in those days, that kind of thing was allowed.

I grew up around the plants and producers, going up to the sierra to see the grows. Back then, [cannabis] seemed very powerful to me. By the time I was born, my dad was already in jail, and my mother was in charge of the family business. But I never knew [cannabis] was "bad." I was very curious when I would see my dad

Miguel Fernández at the 2022 Global Marijuana March in favor of cannabis legalization and regulation in Mexico City.

smoking—even when we went to see him in prison, he would have his own marijuana!

I became interested in activism when they sentenced my mom to ten years in jail on the charge of transportation of marijuana with intent to sell—it was the maximum sentence in her case. She wound up serving six years. I was seventeen years old, and [my] world came crashing down. I lost my job, and the rest of our family told me, "You can't do this work anymore because you're going to wind up in prison!"

Why Don't I Do It Differently?

They were six really difficult years for myself and for my family. At first, I left the marijuana business, but then I asked myself, "Why do I have to leave behind something that is my passion?" Something clicked, and I was like, "Why don't I do it differently? What if I start sharing information?" That way, I wouldn't be doing something that could send me to jail. Well, that's what I thought at the time.

What we did at Xochipilli [Mexico's first public club for cannabis consumers] was about educating people and providing a space to consume without state persecution. In addition to the smoking lounge, we had a radio studio, a medicinal cannabis clinic, recreational areas, a game table, workshops, et cetera. It became a very iconic space in Mexico City for the cannabis community. The thing Mexican cannabis consumers are most in need of are places to smoke. Because many times, if you don't have the privilege of owning a property, you're not going to be able to [safely consume cannabis without fear of law enforcement]. That affects people who still live with their parents and students who have a lot of roommates. In Mexico City the apartments can be really small [so your neighbors can detect smoke].

Who's Down?

We started out [occupying the plaza in front of the Senate building] on Tuesdays and Thursdays in shifts. We would organize ourselves through Facebook chat. One or two people would say, "We have to put the [information] table out this Tuesday. Who's down?" The people who responded would participate. Once we set up the table, we'd talk to passersby about cannabis prohibition. When we started to get more organized, every Tuesday and Thursday our schedule would fill up with workshops, cultural activities, even music.

We were [smoking cannabis publicly] from the very beginning! And in November of 2019, we had this idea: "What would happen if we set up a marijuana plantón permanently?"

We're Not Going Anywhere!

Right now in Mexico City alone, there are at least ten other plantóns, including those made by feminists, newspaper unions, and Indigenous groups. In other countries, protesters rest at night. But here, it's like, "We're not going anywhere until you fix this!"

In November 2019, we alerted the government of our plans and we did an event where we walked from the Senate to the Angel of Independence. [The Angel is one of Mexico City's most iconic monuments and is depicted in the capital's official logo.] That's where we did the first public planting of a cannabis plant.

Even though we alerted the government, they didn't pay us much attention. They were like, "Oh, it's only a plant."

But we told them, "If you take this plant away, we're going to come back double." So then we planted two plants at the Angel of Independence, then four, then eight, then sixteen—and each time, someone would take them away. When we got to thirty-two plants, we decided to erect the plantón in Plaza Luis Pasteur.

We had a planting ceremony and made a public declaration. It was February 2, 2020. We were going to stay put to take care of those plants, in public.

The First Day of the Plantón

That was a very stressful day for me because I had to be there to receive the thirty-two plants from volunteers. I was by myself at first, because everyone else was in a march that was headed towards the plaza. I was like, "Man, they're going to arrest me and everything's gonna go to hell." But finally, people began to arrive in the plaza—stoners always arrive late—and we collected the thirty-two plants that we needed for the permanent planting. We held a ceremony with medicinal marijuana patients, their parents, and other people from the cannabis community. There were about forty of us there that day.

We Now Have a Dog and a Rooster

About twelve [people stayed that first night]. Some people decided to stay and live there, to take care of the plants. I would stay sometimes, but I would be on guard duty [instead of sleeping in the camp].

[Spending the night there] is a trip. People try to break in, steal stuff. Drunk people come by. If it's your turn to be on guard duty, you have to be alert. And—this is strange—but on one side of Plaza Luis Pasteur, there is a really loud pedestrian walk sign. You can deal with that sound when you're only hearing it for a few moments. But when you hear it twenty-four hours a day, it becomes really frustrating. A lot of us dream about that sound because we've been hearing it for two years. There is a lot of chaos at night, especially around dawn. But what has helped us a lot with that are the plantón's animals. We now have a dog and a rooster. The rooster wakes up around 3 a.m., and the dog, if he hears a sound or smells someone who shouldn't be there, he wakes up quick and barks at them.

A Utopia, a Mini City

We have four demands: free cultivation, free possession, shared spaces, and treatment with dignity. What we are saying to the government is this: "If you don't grant our demands, we're going to stay here and care for these plants. We'll see who gives in first." The risk that we ran every day was that they could arrest us, raid us, take away the plants, accuse us of selling drugs. But the Mexico City government has been careful in dealing with us. In fact, there was an entire year in which they didn't interact with the camp. Even the police would go by the plantón pretending like they didn't see us. It was really crazy—it was a utopia, a mini city, where the police didn't enter, and where the government ignored us. Later on, the plantón became so large that they couldn't ignore it. At that point, the government had to negotiate. Since then, we've liberated two more spaces, one in front of the Supreme Court and one in front of Congress.

These Are Protest Plants

On Tuesdays and Thursdays, there are volunteers working in the cannabis garden. Visitors can learn about the plants and work with the volunteers. On Saturdays, we have the Popular School of Cannabis Activism [Escuela Popular de Activismo Cannábico, which shares skills with cannabis activists from across the country]. We have a women's group, and sometimes sound systems will play music. If there's no activities going on, we give visitors a tour of the space and explain how they can collaborate. At this point, the camp is kind of like a mini commune. There's a bathroom that was built from wood and connects to the sewer. There's a kitchen, the office we work in, the cultivation classroom where we keep the plants. Right now, there are five tents where people sleep. We've never had more than ten sleeping tents. In the two years in which the plantón has existed, we've cultivated more than ten thousand plants. The camp is full of pots, tennis shoes with plants growing in them. We've tried to put plants everywhere and gift seeds to people so they can cultivate in their own homes. But these are protest plants; the goal is not to smoke them. Honestly, there's a lot of pests and fungus on the plants in the camp, which is hard to control. For the purposes of education, there are various garden sections and various teaching styles. There's the closet, where we do interior and hydroponic cultivation. There are also some terraces where we grow corn and other vegetables.

Beginning to Understand

In Mexico City, if you ask marijuana consumers—before the plantón existed—if they'd ever seen a weed plant, which I would do a lot in workshops, even people who consume would say no! But when they see the living plants, it normalizes the idea that this is—yeah, a plant. And a living being. For people who don't consume, it's a reckoning: "This thing that I'm looking at is the thing that is so prohibited?" And if a person is curious, that makes the person want to know more. Seeing the plant has been very important in the public's process of beginning to understand that the cannabis community isn't full of criminals, like older people sometimes think.

Definitely an Achievement

Even if we're still fighting on a federal level for a comprehensive law that defends cannabis consumer rights, the plantón has managed to normalize the plant on a massive scale. When we have a

CHAPTER 14
A Tool for Fighting Racism and Sexism

Luana Malheiro, Anthropologist and Anti-Prohibition Activist

I t is impossible to understand the fight for cannabis rights in Brazil without first learning a little about the drug's history in Africa, an ancestral homeland of most Brazilians. Africa is one of the birthplaces of modern cannabis culture. North Africans have been documented using the drug for its psychoactive properties as far back as the eleventh century. People from the continent's eastern regions have been smoking psychoactive marijuana in pipes since at least the 1300s, longer than anywhere else in the world. Many historians give credit to the Africans who were kidnapped, forced into slavery, and brought to the Western Hemisphere between the 1500s and 1800s for bringing psychoactive cannabis consumption to the land that came to be known as the Americas. Though little early documentation exists of psychoactive cannabis use in western Africa, where many enslaved people came from, it seems that some brought cannabis seeds with them on the arduous Middle Passage, in addition to okra, yams, watermelon, and black-eyed peas. They found that marijuana—which has painkilling and stress-relieving effects—could be an important therapeutic tool in withstanding the brutal physical labor of slavery. By the mid-nineteenth century, four million enslaved Africans had been sent to Brazil, then a colony of Portugal.

In the 1800s, Black people in Brazil also consumed cannabis during spiritual rites tied to African faiths. White colonial society did not approve and sought to link these practices with criminality, mental decline, the weakening of family bonds, and even devil worship. In 1830 Rio de Janeiro became the first municipality in the world to ban the sale and consumption of marijuana. Residents who used the drug—then mainly African—faced jail time, while the dealers (usually white apothecary owners) were merely fined. Colonists wrote into law racist bans on other Black cultural practices, including the musical martial art capoeira, samba dancing, and African religious rites. By 2021 Afro-Brazilians made up 56 percent of Brazil's population, and cannabis continued to be a drug characterized by its Black roots. Linguists have connected maconha and diamba, common Brazilian words for cannabis, to the Kimbundu language of Angola.

Modern-day Brazilian people from all racial groups buy and sell cannabis and other drugs, and in 2017, the first cannabis-based medicine was approved for legal sale. But drug policing is as racially biased as it was back in the nineteenth century, and the government continues to use it as one of its weapons to control Black and other marginalized communities. One study at a prison in southern Brazil found that incarcerations for drug trafficking increased 427 percent between 2006 and 2015. By 2015, the country's total prison population had increased by 170 percent over the course of fifteen years. In 2020 Brazilian police killed more than 6,416 people—almost six times more than the total number of people murdered by United States police during that time, despite the much larger US population. Far Right president Jair Bolsonaro, who was in office from 2019 to 2022, was seen as being at the heart of this uptick in arrests and police violence. He was an enthusiastic supporter of bloody police raids on alleged drug dealers, largely in the Afro-Brazilian neighborhoods called

Brazilian favelas, such as Cantagalo in Rio de Janeiro, have been at the epicenter of police brutality related to drug enforcement policies.

favelas. In 2022 one such operation resulted in over twenty-eight hundred drug-related arrests in the state of São Paulo. Even self-identified cannabis activists have been targeted. In 2021 police raided medical marijuana organization ABRACannabis, uprooting the cannabis plants meant for patients.

Brazilian anthropologist, mother, anti-prohibition activist, and DJ Luana Malheiro authored a 2020 book in which she explored the lives of eight Brazilian women who use drugs. Her group, National Network of Feminist Antiprohibitionists (RENFA), has built solidarity among activists—largely women of color—to resist discriminatory Drug War policing. Founded in 2016, RENFA has organized protests across the country, including in prisons where many Black women receive draconian sentencing for low-level participation in the country's vast unlicensed drug trade. Malheiro's activism focuses on the uneven ways in which the system targets marginalized groups for violence. Her gender-based analysis is essential in the fight for their well-being, especially since the number of incarcerated Brazilian women quintupled between

2000 and 2014. In a country whose statistics of murders of trans and gender-diverse people are the highest in the world, advocates say that police go out of their way to harm and kill Afro-Brazilian trans women. Though the statistics about violence in cannabis policing are not available, in our 2021 interview, Malheiro makes it clear how stigmatization of marijuana users contributes to a system that puts Black women and their families in danger.

Bolsonaro's time in office came to an end in 2022, when he refused to accept his reelection defeat to leftist former president Luiz Inácio Lula da Silva. Followers of Bolsonaro stormed and sacked the Brazilian Congress and presidential palace in an attack reminiscent of Donald Trump supporters' January 6, 2021, siege on the US Capitol. Afterwards, Lula questioned whether military police were complicit with the Bolsonaro supporters. "There was an explicit connivance of the police with the demonstrators," said the elected president. Time will tell how the new presidential election deals with law enforcement corruption, and the violence against drug workers and advocates of which Malheiro spoke in our interview.

LUANA MALHEIRO

My Father Found My Joints

At the age of eighteen, I was committed by my parents to an inpatient addiction rehabilitation facility. I had been smoking marijuana on the weekends, but I had never consumed it on a daily basis. My dad and mom didn't have a lot of education on the subject. They have worked in the fields most of their lives and live in a rural area where there's not much understanding of the consumption of substances besides beer and liquor. I stayed in rehab for three months, and it was brutal.

I told them [I was using marijuana]. My father had found some of my joints, so I sat down to speak with him and my mother. I don't hold them responsible for what happened to me in the rehab facility. They had no idea what kind of treatment I was getting or of the things that took place there. I was restrained for three days at a time and forced to take pills against my will twice a day for two months. Later, I would find out that the medication they were giving me was capable of causing psychotic breaks. I shared a room with a girl who was given electroshock therapy. The nurses said that if we didn't stay calm, that would happen to us too. It was a moment of horror. A good portion of us there were young marijuana consumers.

Anti-prohibition activist
Luana Malheiro

I went through an intense process in which they tried to humiliate me, and I was the victim of an assault by a young man who worked there. We didn't have the right to read or to speak to other people.

I Didn't Have a Marijuana Problem

Afterwards, I needed time to recuperate. It took me six months to be able to go back to the university, because the effects of those pills were very strong. I couldn't speak well; I couldn't think straight. I think it was in this moment when I woke up to this question of drug consumption, of marijuana consumption. I was absolutely clear on the fact that I didn't have a marijuana problem. It was the reverse. I started consuming marijuana when I was studying for my degree in social sciences at the university, and I was surprised to find that it made me happier and more creative. I began to work within harm reduction causes. The work helped me, because when I got out of rehab, I developed a compulsive consumption of other substances. Knowing about harm reduction gave me direction. Later, I would do harm reduction work in the context of electronic music parties, where I also worked as a DJ or at the door of the event. We had an educational area for drug users within the event and a team of health students who provided drug analysis services. I later began to work with homeless women, men, and children who consumed substances. Through that work, and also from my experiences from living in a neighborhood where there was a lot of police abuse and violence, I came to understand the problems that are generated by prohibitionist systems.

Women Who Are Survivors of War

Cannabis prohibition, and the prohibition of drugs in general, have generated a violent situation in our country for women. RENFA was created by women who are survivors of war—that's how we look at it. Women who were incarcerated, and women who have gotten out of prison. Women who are homeless, women who are no longer homeless. Some of the issues we address are sexual violence against women and against homeless women. Women losing the custody of their children because they are cannabis consumers and consumers of other drugs like cocaine and crack. Some women who use drugs and give birth don't even leave the hospital with their children before their kid is taken away [by child services]. This is a very common situation here in Brazil, and through the lens of feminist activism we are able to raise it for debate. This is our starting point, a debate about women by women.

This Doesn't Happen to White Women

Brazil was the first country to prohibit marijuana. The prohibition of marijuana is a global conspiracy that was not created to fight marijuana but rather [to fight] Black people. Let's keep in mind that white people are certainly involved in the consumption and sales of drugs, but the police don't look into that, and as a result there are no consequences for them. Prohibition is only for Black people in our country. Who are the incarcerated people in Brazil? Black people. Who are the murder victims? Black people—our country's young Black boys. This is not a coincidence. This is a well-structured project created by white supremacy to reinforce the racial hierarchy.

Many Black women can't find work to support their children and families. Often the easiest-to-find job is within the commercial drug market. Women do the worst jobs in those organizations, that of micro-trafficking [selling small amounts of substances, often in the street and public places, which leaves drug workers more exposed], and they often use the money to support their kids. They're also the ones who wind up going to jail, which deeply impacts their communities. There is a relationship between the feminization of poverty and the increase in the incarceration of women. This is a matter that we must view through a racial lens, because this situation doesn't happen to white women.

A Kind of Harry Anslinger Narrative

At the moment, as a law is being considered that would regulate medicinal marijuana in Brazil, the government only [talks about] the bad [health effects of cannabis]. It's a kind of [former US drug czar] Harry Anslinger narrative, you know? That famous prohibitionist. Our government doesn't put out [drug] campaigns based on science. They would rather create this fantasy that marijuana is a substance used by bad people, people who will kill you—very much things that Anslinger said back in his day.

Misinformation about Marijuana Legalization

During this administration specifically, the president has fought quite a bit with members of the press. It's quite striking, because he initiated the practice of speaking about his ideas on YouTube, Instagram, Twitter. He's got quite the digital militia [following him]. They say Bolsonaro has a specific team involved in online dissemination [of propaganda] among young people, among the entire population. They say they use platforms like YouTube, Twitter—the platforms that young people use—to spread misinformation about marijuana legalization. Anti-prohibition activists are in the sights of Bolsonaro.

Another thing that I think is important to understand is that Bolsonaro is a member of the military, one who is involved with retired police officers who make up a paramilitary organization that controls the direction of the drug trade, a group that is in a power struggle with other criminal organizations. Here in Brazil, we had the assassination of Marielle [Franco—see sidebar], who was a great politician who spoke about these issues, about the crimes committed by the police, by the paramilitaries. She denounced the War on Drugs. Her following began to grow in Brazil, and then she was assassinated. Many human rights defenders receive death threats. There have also been more community invasions by the police [during the Bolsonaro administration]. They'll show up shooting, at all hours. There's a very heavy statistic, that this year more than two hundred children under the age of ten were murdered in police operations. [This figure might be much higher. In 2020 the Brazilian Public Security Forum estimated that police killed two children every day.] So we are fighting for a new drug policy in Brazil, but right now we're all more concentrated on getting rid of Bolsonaro. Life for both drug users and anti-prohibition activists is not OK right now in Brazil.

We Had to Make Our Own Collective

[RENFA] got started in 2016. Many of our founding members didn't feel comfortable in other feminist groups. We would bring up the issue of women who use drugs, issues of police rape, and other human rights violations, and those wouldn't be seen as important issues by other feminists—there would be no support. So we began to think that we had to make our own collective to be able to speak about the issues that mattered to us.

We began to hold panel discussions and debates in the streets, in spaces where rapes or incidents of police brutality had taken place. Something that I'm very proud of is that we center our activism in the concept of taking care of each other, because prohibition causes trauma. We think there is another way to formulate

Marielle Franco

Marielle Franco was a politician and sociologist who was serving as a city councillor in Rio de Janeiro when retired law enforcement agents allegedly assassinated her in 2018. Franco was the only Black woman on the city's legislative board at the time. She was openly queer and a full-throated advocate for Brazil's underprivileged communities. Vocal about her opposition to police brutality through both politics and academic research, Franco gained a dedicated political following that has hardly diminished in the years since her death.

Thousands of Brazilians took to the streets in protest following Marielle Franco's assassination, and murals honoring her, such as this one in São Paulo, cropped up throughout the country.

drug policy: with care, with support from feminist groups and antiracist groups. We now have more than five hundred women who are members, and we have organized actions in eleven Brazilian states, even in prisons with incarcerated women and their families. We have held actions with women who are living in the street. We helped to pass a law in [the state of] Bahia that regulates harm reduction. We have made it our mission to approach other social movements, like housing rights groups, feminist groups, Afro groups. We want to begin a movement of Latin American and Caribbean anti-prohibitionist feminists, with the idea that this is a global problem. We believe that we have this mission, to create a new political formulation from the base of our own stories, our lives, our trajectories, and also from the union of our different trajectories.

Respect Our Culture, Our Sovereignty, Our Rights

[Readers should know,] first of all, that the United States has a big responsibility in all this. There's no way of explaining global drug policy without talking about North American imperialism, and without talking about the sovereignty [that has been taken away from] our [Latin American and Caribbean] countries. We have the right to create our own policies in accordance with our cultures, with our lived experiences, with our histories. Respect our culture, our sovereignty, our rights.

We have to struggle, all of us together, for a drug policy that guarantees justice for all. We believe in a drug legalization that repairs—if repair is possible—the harms that have been done to communities. We have to support and not punish drug users. We want them living, debating with us. We are here because of all these people, because of all the women, who are incarcerated and who cannot speak for themselves like I am now. We are here for our assassinated companions, even for those who we didn't know.

CHAPTER 15

A Way to Learn about Global Politics

Froylán Rascón, Former Participant and Staff Member of an International Drug Education Program

Catalyst is an educational program for young people that seeks to bust myths and misinformation surrounding the international War on Drugs. It was founded in 2015 as an in-person, three-week course in Mexico City and Tepoztlán. Teens from across the American continents gathered to take classes that utilized their own experiences with drug prohibition as a taking-off point. In teaching about how prohibition impacts students' communities, Catalyst's curriculum underlines the global interconnectedness of the illegal drug industry and its policing. Lesson plans encourage participants to think about political situations and events influenced by the industry, such as the United States' extensive prison-industrial complex, and coca-producing Colombia's unending civil war, which has killed more than 260,000 people and displaced over 8 million—including nearly 74,000 individuals in 2021 alone.

As of 2023, the organization provides materials to educators interested in engaging young people in a critical and transnational analysis of drug policy. Catayst's lesson plans are available in both Spanish and English and are compatible with many curriculums, even online teaching.

Here's an example of how Catalyst teaches: One lesson addresses the ways that international forces of supply and demand affect the transportation and distribution of illegal psychoactive substances. To do this, the lesson plan guides students to research the foods they ate for breakfast. Where were the ingredients for your cereal grown? What can you learn about the workers that helped produce it? How far did your cereal travel to make it to your bowl? Are you comfortable with where the dollars used to buy your morning meal went? The lesson goes on to parallel the journey of your cereal with the economy that creates and sells drugs. That means that the inequities of the War on Drugs reflect the problems of global society. Drug economies are as much a part of our world as the capitalist system that brings us our cornflakes.

Froylán Rascón went through the in-person Catalyst course as a high school student in Mexico. He loved the program so much that he remained connected to Catalyst long after, eventually

Students in the Catalyst program participate in a learning activity as part of their classwork in 2019.

becoming an intern and then social media manager for the organization. He believes that learning about international drug policy and the economy is the key to young people's ability to understand—and change—the world.

FROYLÁN RASCÓN

That Just Say No Kind of Education

My education about drugs was very poor. In elementary school, they definitely didn't teach us anything about them. In middle school, they only talked to us about neurotransmitters. Like, "If you do cocaine, this is what happens in your neurons, et cetera." But they never talked to us about harm reduction.

What we *did* experience in school was tremendous criminalization. In my middle school, there were already young people who, in the first year, were smoking marijuana and bringing pipes to school. That kind of behavior was seen as delinquent. I had one friend who they expelled for smoking, and they were about to expel me for it as well. Even in middle school, marijuana was always present. Our school director wanted to criminalize it, keep it taboo, and stigmatize the consumption of substances. It's always been that Just Say No kind of education. Like, "If they offer you drugs, say no." "Individuals who use drugs are criminals and bad people." "Don't use drugs!" That was my drug education.

Understand, Rethink, and Redefine

Catalyst is a pedagogical [teaching] initiative that looks to unite young people from all over the American continents to rethink and discuss drug policy, primarily that of their own countries. But the program keeps in mind that ultimately, drug policy is regional. So the idea of Catalyst is to bring young people together to understand, rethink, and redefine these local and regional policies that affect them.

I was an activist in high school, and I was putting on political and cultural activities with a group of friends and classmates. A friend of mine who knew Camila Ruiz Segovia, the codirector of Catalyst at that time, shared an announcement with me that said the program was looking for participants.

When I first heard about Catalyst, I thought, "What an incredible opportunity!" At the time, I was very interested in other subjects related to the global War on Drugs, including how the consumption of substances in Mexico, and in general, have structural repercussions. I was already thinking about those ideas, and being able to attend Catalyst really opened doors for me in terms of deepening my thinking about drug politics.

What Is Happening?

The moment that stands out in my mind, the one that made me think "What is happening?" and "I want to understand this better!" was in 2014, when forty-three students from Ayotzinapa Rural Teachers' College disappeared. Investigations turned up information that pointed to the students' disappearance having been due to the fact that one of their school buses was carrying a secret cargo of poppy sap [which is often used to make opiate drugs]. That's one of the hypotheses for why they were arrested and then disappeared.

From there I was like, "Damn! Drugs are involved in everything." From that point on, I wanted to start building new paths with other young people and [I believed] that drugs had to be present in our thoughts about those new paths.

The Session

The 2018 session of Catalyst took place over two weeks in the town of Tepoztlán, Morelos, in Mexico, in a very beautiful house.

We talked and took classes and workshops, and then for another week we were in Mexico City. That's where we presented the program's results.

[The other participants were from] Canada, the United States, Mexico, Costa Rica, Guatemala, Honduras, Peru, Paraguay—I think that's it.

Participants' Experiences

I think that the most relevant factor [in understanding the War on Drugs] had to do with the socioeconomic gap and access to rights. Of course, our New York peer was not going to understand things in the same way as our peer from Colombia's Cauca Valley, you know? I mean, both have experienced the consequences of the War on Drugs in their communities, but for example, our peer from Cauca Valley didn't speak English, which was the case with a lot of our coursemates. The majority of the program participants came from Colombia, if I'm remembering correctly, and the majority didn't speak English, which wasn't a huge problem. It was evident that the Colombian education system has its deficiencies when compared with that of the United States or Mexico.

Our classmate from New York knew a lot about racism, xenophobia, homophobia, et cetera. But never in her life had she even heard about, let alone had to face, having armed [military] law enforcement agents stationed in the street by her house or in her school. Our peers from Colombia grew up on a battlefield. So of course, educational access doesn't completely determine Catalyst participants' experiences.

Language and Translation

I think that the Catalyst facilitators did excellent work [with language]. There was simultaneous translation for the entire course. When there was a class or subject that we were learning about in

English, everyone who didn't speak the language put a hearing device on and they got simultaneous Spanish translations. The same thing happened when we were learning in Spanish. The non-Spanish speakers used the same devices for simultaneous English translation.

Other Realities

For me, it was especially shocking coming close to other realities, you know? Despite being from Mexico City and being an activist and having had some experience with the subject of the course, it was shocking and moving to listen to the stories and lived experiences of young people from other parts of the hemisphere. That was a very revealing experience. It opened my eyes and struck me as being very important and significant. Above all, it helped me to understand that we really can't stick to thinking about politics as they relate to just our state or our country. If we're going to make profound changes, they have to happen at the regional or international level. That's what stuck out the most from my experience at Catalyst.

Transform Our Reality Together

Young people are always surrounded by substances. At some point, we're likely to have an experience smoking weed or with another kind of psychedelic substance or even, depending on our context, harder drugs. It's nearly inevitable. And at some moment, if [we're] going to come into contact with them, it's important that we know about drugs in terms of their effects and consequences. Part of that is understanding where they come from and the economic circuit that allows drugs to be present among us.

I personally think that the big structural, social, political, cultural, economic problems that we have in the Americas are always related (and in large part, conditioned) by certain policies. Those include failed security strategies, drug combat, the perpetuation of stigmatizing, criminalizing, poorly informed logic that in large part comes from the United States and spreads south. These factors have turned our countries into war zones

I have a lot of faith and confidence in young people . . . a lot of faith. If we want to transform our reality together, if we want to change it so that we can live in dignity, in a different way from the misery and penury [extreme poverty] that this system has generated, we have to understand the roots of these huge problems. And for me, those have to do with drugs and the policies surrounding them. It's important to know these policies, know where they come from, know who implements them, if we want to change them. When you're young and political, Catalyst's lessons aren't just valuable for when you're studying or analyzing things from a desk. They are tools that help you out in life, that help you to become socially active on a daily basis. So, yes, I'd recommend it to everyone. Especially to restless young people who want to change the reality in which we live.

CHAPTER 16
How Moms Change the World
Ana Álvarez, Cannabis Cultivation Association Founder

H eroic parents around the world have played a seminal role in the legalization of the medical marijuana their kids need. Ana Álvarez of Lima, Peru, deserves her place in the history books. Álvarez is the cofounder and president of Buscando Esperanza (Looking for Hope), a collective of moms who have been cultivating medicinal cannabis for their family members since before it was legal in their country. She learned about cannabis's potential during a search for treatments that could help her son Anthony, who has an intense form of epilepsy. One day, she brewed Anthony a tea made from cannabis. It immediately reduced the severity of his seizures. This astounding turnaround led Álvarez to help form Buscando Esperanza. Soon the group was marching to change their society's perception of cannabis.

It has not been easy. In 2017 authorities charged Álvarez and two other collective members with criminal offenses that could have sent them to jail for fifteen years. But if cops were looking to paint the medical cannabis movement in a criminal light, their actions had the opposite effect. Largely due to the group's work, in 2021 Peruvian pharmacies began selling limited cannabis-based pharmaceuticals, and the country's first medicinal marijuana dispensary opened its doors.

Ana Álvarez (*center*) stands with other activists at a Buscando Esperanza protest.

Buscando Esperanza's fight for cannabis rights continues. They want to expand the law to give families access to the many forms of cannabis medicine that can improve their loved ones' lives. Álvarez says that includes the right to cultivate and process medicinal cannabis at home, and the patients' right to take the kinds of cannabis products they need to get better.

ANA ÁLVAREZ

A Source of Hope

I have a son Anthony, who was born with a degenerative disease called tuberous sclerosis, which caused him to have Lennox-Gastaut syndrome. The neurologist told me that Anthony would get worse, little by little. He was going to lose the ability to speak. Then he wouldn't be able to walk anymore, or study. My job was to focus on giving him the best quality of life possible.

Marijuana Rights for Parents

In 2018 Brooklyn, New York, parent Shakira Kennedy turned to cannabis to deal with the excessive morning sickness she was experiencing during her second pregnancy. She voluntarily told a doctor of this medicinal use. Soon after, child services presented Kennedy with a neglect petition, offering her the choice of attending addiction and parenting classes or losing her kids. Her case was eventually dismissed, but Kennedy went to the press with her story.

Cannabis-consuming parents like her are growing in number, and many refuse to stay silent. More pregnant people are turning to cannabis after experiencing the way it can smooth over the rough parts of gestating a baby, like alleviating nausea. We have yet to see a definitive study that proves pregnant people can harm their fetus by using cannabis—though government health agencies like the National Institute on Drug Abuse counsel pregnant or breastfeeding parents to closely coordinate with their doctor if they plan on consuming marijuana. But a harsh stigma surrounds parents who do weed or other drugs, even after babies are born. Common stereotypes hold that a parent who consumes can't be caring well for their children—an outlook that ignores the many positive effects cannabis can have on the lives of parents.

Kennedy is far from the only parent to stand up to discriminatory drug policy. In 2022 Arizona mom Lindsay Ridgell won her legal appeal against being put on the state's child abuse registry for consuming *legally prescribed* medical cannabis while pregnant, which she found necessary due to extreme morning sickness. Other parents say that they use marijuana post-pregnancy to deal with anxiety that could stand in the way of a calm relationship with their offspring or to help them focus on activities with their kids. Protecting parents and their families against damaging and discriminatory prohibitionist drug policy will likely be a big issue in years to come.

That's how I started living my life between hospitals, medical consultations, and emergencies. Anthony would have convulsions five to ten times a day, which affected his mental health. By the time he was fifteen, he was suffering from a psychiatric crisis. He was losing touch with reality, and even attacked some of his family members. But I didn't want to give up. I started investigating on the internet and came across the case of Charlotte [Figi], a little girl in Colorado who had a similar condition to Anthony. Her family was able to treat her condition with medicinal marijuana. Before this, I had thought marijuana was bad, something negative. I never thought that the plant would be able to help my son. The idea of this treatment became our last alternative, a source of hope.

It was a very long road, but now we have been able to [access this treatment]. Marijuana has been legally recognized as a medicine since 2017 in Peru, although they are still working on the details of the regulation.

Free Access to Health and Dignity

Buscando Esperanza was formed by a group of mothers who were looking to better the quality of life for their children. When I was researching tuberous sclerosis, I met another mother named Dorothy Santiago who also had a child with the disease. We would later meet more mothers who were researching cannabis treatments, and we became convinced that it was our children's best hope. We tried importing medicinal cannabis, but that proved to be too expensive, not to mention illegal. We realized, with professional medical guidance, that we had to start growing the plant ourselves. That's how we formed Buscando Esperanza, whose mission is free access to health and dignity.

We held informational workshops about medicinal marijuana. We showed up at Congress to advocate for our children's right to the plant's medicine. We formed a cultivation collective and began growing cannabis for our kids in an apartment in San Miguel [a neighborhood in Peru's capital city Lima]. That's when the police showed up, in March 2017. The cultivator who was taking care of the plants called me to let me know that the police had entered the apartment, and that they had informed him that they were going to take the plants. I got in touch with the other mothers, and we decided that we would defend our cannabis plants.

My Oldest Son Was Sent to Jail

We showed up with protest signs and our children and started camping out. In Latin America, that kind of protest is called a plantón. [For more about plantón protests, see chapter 13.] We sent letters to politicians, to doctors, to government health officials. We organized marches to the health ministry and to the college of oncology. In May of that year, Peru held a march on a global day of cannabis protests, and there, the police beat protesters, shot us with tear gas, and put parents in jail—even my oldest son was sent to jail. But I think that's when the officials realized that this group of people really needed this plant. That's where the first medicinal marijuana law in Peru came from. It didn't happen immediately, but our protests led to government legalizing the importation of medicinal marijuana and its sale through laboratories and pharmacies.

However, that's not what we wanted. We wanted to be able to cultivate our families' medicine. It hurt that after all that, after they beat us while we were marching, that we hadn't even won the rights we fought for. But we did make political allies, members of Congress who supported us. It was thanks to them that in 2021, Congress approved Law #30861, which legalized cannabis cultivation associations like ours. They're still working on the details of the regulations, but it's the law that we fought for, for so many years.

I Still Face a Lot of Discrimination

Peru is a very conservative country, and I would say that many hypocrites live here. For example, I still face a lot of discrimination, even from my own neighbors. I now grow my son's cannabis in my apartment, and the building association has even installed security cameras to see who comes and goes from my home, keeping an eye on me. We still need so much education about cannabis here in Peru, especially since the police can still arrest you for its possession. If that happens, you have to hire a lawyer to prove that it's for medicinal purposes.

I Owe So Much to Cannabis

Anthony has been taking medicinal cannabis since 2015, and it has improved his quality of life by quite a lot. He's twenty-two years old and has been able to participate in society, even socialize with friends. He wasn't able to do that before beginning cannabis treatment because his seizures had left him with brain damage that made him aggressive and unable to concentrate. Now, he's been able to take part in workshops where he does theater, painting, baking—he even has his own project where he makes nutritious desserts. It's incredible, you have to see it to believe it.

I owe so much to cannabis, and I will always defend it. It has allowed my family to have mental, emotional, and economic peace. I'm not alone. I've met so many families with children who also have neurological conditions who have benefited from this medicine. Dorothy, the other mothers of Buscando Esperanza, and I always say, "It was all worth it—all the marches, all the sacrifices." It's cost us many tears, you understand? But now people benefit from that work. Patients call us and tell us about how their health has improved, how they can do things now that they never could before. You can't put a price on that. You can't put a price on health.

CHAPTER 17
Groundbreaking Politics

Diego Olivera, Former Secretary-General of Uruguay's National Drug Commission

W hat must happen for a country to go all in on equitable cannabis legalization? The answer varies, but for one example, we can turn to Uruguay. The country, tucked into the geographic junction of Brazil, Argentina, and the South Atlantic Ocean, has a population smaller than that of Los Angeles. Uruguay made history in 2013 by becoming the first nation in the modern era to legalize the sale of cannabis for both recreational and medicinal uses. Canada would be next to legalize recreational sales, but not until five years later. Other countries have since decriminalized some form of marijuana possession, cultivation, or both, including Jamaica, Czech Republic, Mexico, Colombia, and Belize. But for a while, Uruguay was out there on its own, making up the rules for nationwide legal weed.

So perhaps it's no surprise that the country's system for growing and selling marijuana turned out to be unique. Although legalization is often the goal of cannabis advocates, the governmental act of legalizing weed hardly tells the whole story about how people will be allowed to interact with the drug. What *kind* of legalization is important. How much cannabis is a person allowed to have at one time? Where can it be consumed? Who is allowed to grow and sell the plant? What kind of products can be made with weed? Can the drug be sold, and if so, where do the profits go? What measures have been established to make sure that the communities targeted by Drug War policing can profit from the marijuana industry once it is legal, and how effective have those measures been? It's important to clock the answers to these questions, because they can make the difference between social equity and accessible medicine, a green-washed corporate cash grab, or any of the other realities from making legal a substance that was once prohibited.

In Uruguay the progressive 2010–2015 government of President José Mujica put together a system that prioritizes people growing their own cannabis, cultivating it in groups called cannabis clubs, or buying it from government-licensed pharmacies. This kind of state-driven cannabis legalization doesn't prioritize the profits of big business. In fact, barely any large companies and no foreign entities are allowed to participate in Uruguay's cannabis industry.

When Uruguay legalized cannabis, it did more than destigmatize and widen access to marijuana or even drugs in general. The government corrected law enforcement and health policies that had been in effect for eons but that had been the source of injustice and violence toward the people they were meant to protect.

I learned a lot about this key chapter in cannabis history from interviewing Diego Olivera, a government official who oversaw Uruguay's bold move to legalize the drug. Building on his background as a youth social worker, Olivera helped develop programs to expand not only access to cannabis but also an understanding of the drug.

DIEGO OLIVERA

My Path to Cannabis Policy

I was a young university student at the end of the millennium. At that time, young people were bringing a lot of energy to the idea that prohibition had failed, and that at least with cannabis, there had to be a change. But in that moment [cannabis legalization] was seen as a young person's insanity.

[After college] I began to work with homeless kids and teens. In 2002 Uruguay, along with the rest of the global south, went through a very serious economic crisis that caused our poverty rates to explode. We are a country with a history of strong social policies compared with other places in Latin America. But that model began to crack in the 1990s and

Diego Olivera, cannabis official

wound up exploding, one could say, in the 2000s. Even though later we were able to recover, it was a moment in which our society got much poorer. One of the most visible signs of that poverty was more and more homeless children.

As a social worker, I came into contact with one of the most serious problems facing homeless young people, which was the [problematic] consumption of substances. Those were the circumstances through which I began to work—not with cannabis but with major issues surrounding other drugs and, in particular, their consumption by people suffering from social exclusion. That work made it possible for me to see how wrong prohibitionist politics were. Drug users were seen as something to be feared, something dangerous. These kids were finding it impossible to find help within the state's health system.

In 2016, after working on a variety of social assistance programs, I was invited to become secretary-general of the National Drug Commission. I think the principal factor behind why I was chosen to be secretary is because at the time, I was thirty-six years old. I belonged to a generation that could understand legalization and could, in some way, bring it forward.

Respecting and Defending Individual Liberties

I don't think there is just one answer [to why Uruguay was the first country to legalize cannabis]. There are a few factors that have to do with the country's history. Uruguay is a society with a lot of trust in its institutions. Early on in the twentieth century, the Constitution of 1918 separated church from state. In some ways, this gave Uruguay a reputation as a pioneering country. There is the idea that the state has to be present, yes, but also that it has to be present in respecting and defending individual liberties. Our country has never criminalized the consumption of drugs—no one has ever had to go to jail for merely consuming a substance. Our government has always respected the individual's right to decide whether or not to consume. However, you were not allowed to cultivate, buy, or manufacture drugs.

A Way of Controlling Violence

What happened in the years leading up to legalizing cannabis is that Uruguay's historically low murder rate began to rise. A conversation began about why there was so much violence and about what causes homicide. One of the explanations that emerged was that much of the violence was related to the drug trade. Legalization here didn't begin with a consideration of individual liberties or personal rights. Rather, it was a way of controlling violence. The idea was that the drug trade produces much more harm than the drugs themselves, and so it would be better to just regulate drugs. President José Mujica proposed cannabis legalization in 2012, and different groups—students, professionals, political parties—began to declare themselves for or against legalization.

Those who were against it used the same arguments that you can find in any part of the world: that drug consumption would go up among young people, that it would lessen what we call the "perception of risk" around taking drugs—which is to say that it would affect the way that people think of drugs—and that addiction rates would rise, that public health would deteriorate, and that marijuana legalization would lead people to consume other, more dangerous drugs. Luckily, none of these predictions have come to pass.

We Have to Try

The debate was complicated because Uruguay was to be the first country to legalize cannabis. We couldn't say, "They already did this in Mexico or Spain, and it worked." The people who defended legalization focused on the list of harms that prohibition had caused. One thing that helped change people's minds was the case of Alicia Castillo, a sixty-year-old woman who had six cannabis plants growing behind her house. Someone saw them, reported her, and she wound up in jail. That was one moment in which people realized that [cannabis prohibition] wasn't just putting big-time criminals in jail—it was incarcerating people whose only crime was cultivating a plant in their garden. Mujica was a political leader who really knew how to speak to people. What he basically said was, "What we know is that prohibition didn't work. Uruguay has the right to try an alternative, and if this alternative doesn't work, we can turn back. But we have to try."

Weed

Three Routes of Access

Uruguay's system is subject to strict regulations, and it is not very friendly to the free market. There are three routes of access to marijuana. One is home cultivation—adults have the right to grow up to six cannabis plants. You can't sell it, but you can share. The people who live with you can also consume what you produce, or even the people who visit you. Your friends and family can take your marijuana with them, there's no problem with that. But there are no economic transactions allowed.

Then you have the marijuana clubs. They're not businesses; they're civil associations formed by people to cultivate cannabis and distribute what they cultivate amongst themselves. Clubs can grow up to ninety-nine plants and have up to forty-five members, which is still a very small size if you consider all the effort that it takes to form such an organization. The third route is public sales, which can only take place in pharmacies.

All of this is overseen by the Institute for Regulation and Control of Cannabis (IRCCA), which is the governmental agency that creates cannabis regulations and hands out licenses for all three routes of access. There are only a few businesses that have licenses to produce marijuana for commercial pharmacy sales in Uruguay, and they have to be located on a single property that is administered by the IRCCA. That property is 60 kilometers [37 miles] from our capital Montevideo, in the state of San José, in a city named Libertad.

You can't advertise the consumption or sale of cannabis. Edibles are not allowed, unless you make them yourself at home—the same goes for cannabis extractions and concentrations. And you can't participate in more than one of these three routes of access. That is to say, if you chose home cultivation and your supply runs out, or if your plants die, you have to cancel your home cultivation registration and join a club or register for public sale. The system has some "Big Brother" characteristics, if you will. The state controls and supervises everything.

Medicinal Marijuana

The health department in Uruguay has only regulated the medicinal use of pharmaceutical products, such as droppers of CBD concentrate—no cannabis flower or THC products. You have to have a prescription for approved products. But nonetheless, many people use "recreational" cannabis to feel better. The line there is a little blurry.

When the Veil of Prohibition Was Lifted

When the law was passed, only a third of the population was in favor—that is low for a law. But today, about 48 percent of Uruguay is in favor of cannabis legalization, and 7 percent isn't opposed or in favor, but at least they're not bothered by it. For that to have happened in only nine years is really dramatic.

I don't think [that change] came from the politicians. Public perception changes due to day-to-day factors. The War on Drugs created this idea that drug users are irrepressible, dangerous, potentially criminal. That meant some people may have thought that when you go to a pharmacy that sells cannabis, consumers would be sprawled out in the doorway, desperate for their cannabis, or that they would be violent. But when the veil of prohibition was lifted, you were able to see who the people were who produced and consumed cannabis, and they were people as varied and diverse as our society itself. Those prejudices began to collapse.

The economy also played a role. Say for example, you were a senior who may have been frightened by cannabis legalization, and your grandchild begins to work in hemp production. They're doing well, hemp becomes a source of prosperity for them and for your family—your views may change on the subject.

There were also the drug's medicinal uses. Many people, particularly those of an advanced age who may have been the least convinced about legalization, began to use cannabis to control their anxiety, to sleep better, or to manage chronic pain in their joints or their back. When they saw that there were benefits, people began to have a much more natural connection with cannabis, especially compared to what they had been made to believe before, that it was something dangerous.

No Longer a Dirty Word

The ability to grow up in a society where cannabis is not a motive for legal persecution means that we're able to talk about it in a more open and relaxed way. That includes in educational institutions, where we're no longer speaking about cannabis as though it was a dirty word. Young people are much more intelligent when it comes to cannabis, because they have much more information. But there are still social inequities. Low-income communities continue to suffer from the impacts of the drug trade. Uruguayan society—and I think that this goes for all of Latin America— needs to make sure that cannabis legalization benefits low-income young people. There are barriers for young adults in being able to work for the legal cannabis industry, to start cannabis businesses, even in being able to buy legal cannabis.

Required Drug Education

The law that legalized cannabis had special articles that required the school system to educate about drug use. [The National Drug Commission] put together a program that was called Dale Vos [Give It to You], which basically gave teachers didactic games and tools that allowed young people to express themselves. Drug education had always been very top-down and limited to telling young people that using or selling drugs is bad.

What we are trying to do now is teach the teachers to give the kids space in which they can talk about their fears, their concerns, what they know about drugs. Many times, young people know more than their teachers do. And educators have to be able to get past the barrier of their own ignorance to be able to air these issues among their students. It's often as if the adolescent drug user becomes a lost cause, or a reason to call the police or a psychiatrist. We try to give educational institutions the tools they need so that they can manage the subject in the best way possible—and above all, not expel the students who consume drugs. Because when young people who consume substances find the doors of educational institutions closed to them, they become all the more vulnerable to much greater harms.

An Invitation to Talk

And finally, we put together television campaigns. The first one was focused on two ideas: one, that it was true that marijuana has its health risks that are important to know about, but two, that we're a lot safer if it's legal. Then there was a second campaign in which, for example, we'd have a scene in which Mom and Dad are cooking and the kids show up and they ask, "Dad, Mom, have you guys ever used marijuana?" The parents would be confused about how to respond. These ads were meant to serve as an invitation for families to talk about drugs in their homes. We realized that when adults didn't communicate with their children, there was a higher number of problematic situations related to consumption. In families where there was more open communication about drugs, there were fewer cases of problematic use. Parental involvement is a protection factor for young people. There are people who will only accept depictions of marijuana that have to do with illness, danger, death. But in reality, it's much more complex than that.

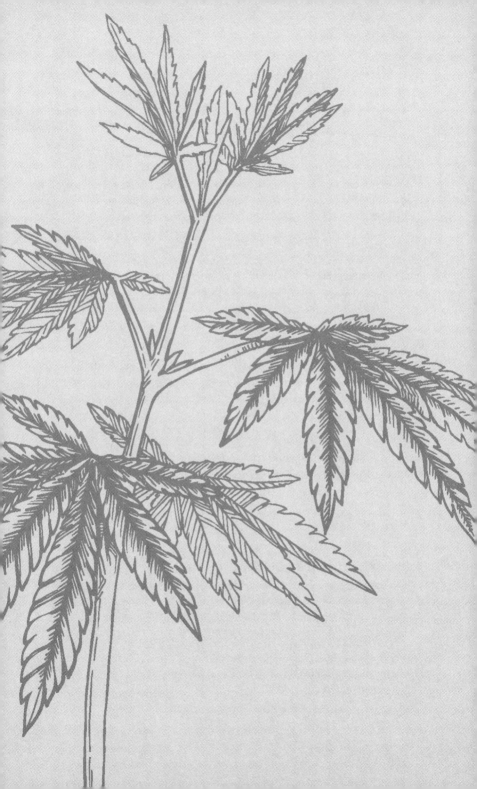

Acknowledgments

First off, many thanks to the young people who helped guide my investigation for this book: Jaden, Sofia, Froylán, Brahian, your testimony on what is and isn't being taught in schools today about drugs—and what teens need to know that is not included in these lessons—was invaluable. I am deeply indebted to my interviewees, who took a chance on an unconventional journalist and YA book concept and spoke frankly about uses of a drug that, in some cases, is still illegal where they live. My work would not be possible without the support of my international cannabis community. My weed madrina Polita Pepper, Zara Snapp, Mary Carreon, Clydeen McDonald, Felicia Carbajal, Jocelyn Padgett, Roxana Poggiolini, Douglas Gordon, and Stephen Clarke provided references that allowed me to connect with brilliant cannabis experts from across the hemisphere. To Oscar Morales for his enthusiasm and excellent Spanish language transcriptions that sharpened my understanding of each conversation. To my editor Ashley Kuehl, who also worked on my first book, for her compassionate communication and for making another of my projects infinitely more readable for young audiences. To my parents, Barbara and Peter, thank you for giving me the space to draw my own conclusions and the unconditional support necessary for one to write about "taboo" subjects without fear. To Olga Rodríguez, my forever roommate, for translation and editorial guidance, but mainly for building a loving home with me during some otherwise insane years. To Amado, mi amor, for holding me down with superhuman patience and endless kitty WhatsApp stickers. And finally, to my familiar Kiara, who should get a coauthor credit for all the time she spent sleeping on my wrists as I tried to type these pages. It's all for you, Kiki—but you knew that.

Source Notes

56   Jones, Matt. "Nick Diaz Reacts to Drug Suspension, UFC Star's Lawyer Confirms Intent to Appeal." Bleacher Report. Bleacher Report, September 27, 2017. https://bleacherreport.com/articles/2566884-nick-diaz-reacts-to -drug-suspension-ufc-stars-lawyer-confirms-intent-to-appeal.

56   Nate Diaz Vapes Marijuana (CBD) at UFC 202 Press Conference. YouTube. YouTube, 2016. https://www.youtube.com/watch?v=1u3rf92rAgw.

130   Cox, Ashley. "Brazilian President Lula Criticizes Police for Protesters' Breach of Government Buildings." CBS News. CBS Interactive, January 10, 2023. https://www.cbsnews.com/tampa/news/brazilian-president -lula-criticizes-police-for-protesters-breach-of-government-buildings/.

Bibliography

Introduction

Guangpeng, Ren, Xu Zhang, Ying Li, Kate Ridout, Martha L. Serrano-Serrano, Yongzhi Yang, Al Liu et al. "Large-Scale Whole-Genome Resequencing Unravels the Domestication History of *Cannabis sativa*." *Science Advances* 7, no. 29 (July 16, 2021). https://www.science.org/doi/10.1126/sciadv.abg2286#con1.

Ives, Mike. "Where Does Weed Come From? A New Study Suggests East Asia." *New York Times*, July 18, 2021. https://www.nytimes.com/2021/07/18/science/asia-marijuana-cannabis-weed.html.

Taylor, Amiah. "Black Cannabis Entrepreneurs Account for Less Than 2% of the Nation's Marijuana Businesses." *Fortune*, April 26, 2022. https://fortune.com/2022/04/26/black-cannabis-entrepreneurs-marijuana-businesses-marijuana-laws/.

Chapter 1: A Drug We Have to Talk About
Emily Jenkins

Abraham, Roshan. "'Safety First' Drug Education Program Acknowledges the Failings of 'Just Say No.'" *Next City*, June 17, 2021. https://nextcity.org/urbanist-news/safety-first-drug-education-program-acknowledges-the-failings-of-saying-no.

American Psychological Association. "Zero Tolerance Policies Are Not as Effective as Thought in Reducing Violence and Promoting Learning in School, Says APA Task Force." Press release, August 2006. https://www.apa.org/news/press/releases/2006/08/zero-tolerance.

Corcione, Adryan. "Black and Brown Teens Are Still More Likely to Be Punished for Smoking Weed." *Teen Vogue*, April 20, 2020. https://www.teenvogue.com/story/420-marijuana-suspend-expel-black-brown-teens.

———. "Connecticut's Adult-Use Marijuana Legalization Protects Youth, Students." Filter, June 23, 2021. https://filtermag.org/connecticut-marijuana-legalization-bill-youth-students/.

———. "Even When Marijuana Is Legal, Young People Are Locked Up for It." Truthout, April 20, 2021. https://truthout.org/articles/even-when-marijuana-is-legal-young-people-are-locked-up-for-it/.

Hart, Carl. *Drug Use for Grown Ups: Chasing Liberty in the Land of Fear*. New York: Penguin Books, 2021.

Iati, Marisa. "A 'Sesame Street' Character's Mom Has an Addiction. Experts Say That's a Valuable Lesson." *Washington Post*, October 12, 2019. https://www .washingtonpost.com/education/2019/10/12/sesame-street-characters-mom -has-an-addiction-experts-say-thats-valuable-lesson/.

Johnson, Joy, and Barbara Moffat. "Cycles: An Educational Resource Exploring Decision Making and Marijuana Use among Young People." Centre for Addictions Research of BC, University of Victoria, the Helping Schools collection. Accessed May 19, 2022. https://vimeo.com/275288448/5e9020e26e.

Mahr, Krista. "U.S. Drug Overdose Deaths Surpass 107,000 Last Year, Another Record." Politico, May 11, 2022. https://www.politico.com/news/2022 /05/11/drug-overdose-deaths-2021-record-00031709.

McGrath, Michael. "Nancy Reagan and the Negative Impact of the 'Just Say No' Anti-Drug Campaign." *Guardian* (US edition), March 8, 2016. https:// www.theguardian.com/society/2016/mar/08/nancy-reagan-drugs-just-say -no-dare-program-opioid-epidemic.

National Academies of Sciences, Engineering, and Medicine. *The Health Effects of Cannabis and Cannabinoids: The Current State of Evidence and Recommendations for Research.* Washington, DC: National Academies, 2017. https://doi.org /10.17226/24625.

Retta, Mary. "Is Marijuana Safe? Experts Weigh In on Teen Weed Use." *Teen Vogue*, December 3, 2020. https://www.teenvogue.com/story/is-marijuana-safe -experts-weigh-in-on-teen-weed-use.

Rosenbaum, Marsha. "Safety First: Real Drug Education for Teens." Drug Policy Alliance, October 8, 2019. https://drugpolicy.org/resource/safety-first -real-drug-education-teens.

Schneider, Keith. "Daryl F. Gates, L.A.P.D. Chief in Rodney King Era, Dies at 83." *New York Times*, April 16, 2010. https://www.nytimes.com/2010/04/17 /us/17gates.html.

Chapter 2: Medicine
Alejo Schroeter and Mariana Ríos

Garcia, Sandra E. "Charlotte Figi, Who Helped Popularize CBD for Medical Use, Dies at 13." *New York Times*, April 9, 2020. https://www.nytimes.com/2020 /04/09/us/charlotte-figi-dead.html.

Grinspoon, Peter. "The Endocannabinoid System: Essential and Mysterious." Harvard Health Publishing, Harvard Medical School, August 11, 2021. https:// www.health.harvard.edu/blog/the-endocannabinoid-system-essential-and -mysterious-202108112569.

Hasse, Javier. "Argentina Regulates Medical Cannabis Self-Cultivation, Sales, Subsidized Access." *Forbes*, November 12, 2020. https://www.forbes.com/sites /javierhasse/2020/11/12/argentina-regulates-medical-cannabis-self-cultivation -sales-subsidized-access/?sh=29db039b1655.

History.com editors. "Marijuana." History, A&E Television Networks. Updated October 10, 2019. https://www.history.com/topics/crime/history-of-marijuana.

Jaeger, Kyle. "House Passes Bipartisan Marijuana Research Bill to Let Scientists Study Dispensary Products, Days after Legalization Vote." Marijuana Moment, April 4, 2022. https://www.marijuanamoment.net/house -passes-bipartisan-marijuana-research-bill-to-let-scientists-study-dispensary -products-days-after-legalization-vote/.

Lee, Martin A. "Endocannabinoid Discovery Timeline." Project CBD, July 1, 2020. https://www.projectcbd.org/science/endocannabinoid-discovery-timeline.

Politi, Daniel. "Argentina to Allow Medicinal Marijuana to Be Grown at Home." *New York Times*. Updated December 11, 2020. https://www.nytimes.com/2020 /11/12/world/americas/argentina-cannabis-marijuana.html.

Singh, Vibha. "Sushruta: The Father of Surgery." *National Journal of Maxillofacial Surgery* 8, no. 1 (January–June 2017): 1–3. https://www.ncbi.nlm.nih.gov/pmc /articles/PMC5512402/.

Wadman, Meredith. "United States Set to Allow More Facilities to Produce Marijuana for Research." *Science*, May 17, 2021. https://www.science.org /content/article/us-set-allow-more-facilities-produce-marijuana-research.

Chapter 3: Food That Makes You Feel Funny
Richard Villegas

Damour, Lisa. "How to Talk to Teens about Edibles." *New York Times*, October 19, 2021. https://www.nytimes.com/2021/10/19/well/family/weed -edibles-teens.html.

"Edibles Dosing: How Strong Is Your Weed Edible?" Leafly. Updated August 12, 2022. https://www.leafly.com/learn/consume/edibles/edible-dosing.

Farah, Troy. "Why Do Edibles Give You a Different High Than Smoking?" *Vice*, February 9, 2018. https://www.vice.com/en/article/bj5mza/edible-high -vs-smoke-high.

"How to Consume Edibles." Leafly. Updated July 14, 2022. https://www.leafly .com/learn/consume/edibles.

Jacoby, Sarah. "Weed Edibles: 8 Things to Know before You Try Ingestible Cannabis Products." *Self*, May 20, 2021. https://www.self.com/story /cannabis-edibles.

Olsen, Morgan. "A First-Timer's Guide to Buying and Using Cannabis Edibles." *Time Out*, April 20, 2021. https://www.timeout.com/usa/things-to-do/first -timers-guide-to-cannabis-edibles.

Taylor, Harry. "Woman Dies in East London after Eating 'Cannabis Sweet.'" *Guardian* (US edition), April 4, 2022. https://www.theguardian.com/uk-news /2022/apr/04/woman-dies-in-east-london-after-eating-suspected-cannabis-sweet.

Chapter 4: Underground Education
Polita Pepper

Associated Press. "Federal Officials Raid Medical Marijuana School in Oakland." *New York Times*, April 2, 2012. https://www.nytimes.com/2012/04/03/us /medical-marijuana-training-school-in-oakland-is-raided.html.

"Cannábicas Documentary." YouTube video. 1:15:23. Posted by Documental Cannábicas, February 27, 2021. https://www.youtube.com/watch?v=czZfbyPoJVc.

Cannativa. YouTube channel. Accessed May 13, 2022. https://www.youtube.com /channel/UCNeL54ZZtGP0c00id4Hac4w.

Donohue, Caitlin. "'Cannábicas' Captures the Struggles of Women in the Global Cannabis Movement." Merry Jane, February 23, 2021. https:// merryjane.com/news/cannabicas-captures-the-struggles-for-women-in-the -global-cannabis-movement.

———. "Mexico's First Ever Weed-Themed TV Show Is about to Debut This Weekend." Merry Jane, February 24, 2021. https://merryjane.com/news /mexicos-first-ever-weed-themed-tv-show-is-about-to-debut-this-weekend.

Hasse, Javier. "The Unusual Suspects: 12 Hispanic Power Players in the Cannabis Space to Watch in 2022." *Forbes*, December 30, 2021. https://www .forbes.com/sites/javierhasse/2021/12/30/forget-the-usual-suspects-12 -hispanic-power-players-in-the-cannabis-space-to-watch-in-2022/.

Munguía, G. Elizabeth. "Cannativa: The Story of a Pioneering Project." *Skunk*, Fall 2021. https://issuu.com/skunkmagazine/docs/skunkfall2021_digital.

Pepper, Polita. "Salió macho: El mundo cannábico también es sexista." *Vice en Español*, August 9, 2018. https://www.vice.com/es/article/qvmeb3/salio-macho -el-mundo-cannabico-tambien-es-sexista.

Chapter 5: A Tool for Athletes
Al Harrington

"Al Harrington and David Stern Talk Medical Marijuana." YouTube video, 14:08. Posted by Uninterrupted, October 25, 2017. https://youtube.com/watch?v=9sVsR2DsFKs.

Barcott, Bruce, Beau Whitney, and Janessa Bailey. "Leafly Jobs Report 2021." Leafly and Whitney Economics. Accessed August 15, 2022. https://leafly-cms-production.imgix.net/wp-content/uploads/2021/02/13180206/Leafly-JobsReport-2021-v14.pdf.

Bobrow, Warren. "Al Harrington, Founder of Viola Cannabis, Digs Deeply into Five Questions." *Forbes*, May 13, 2020. https://forbes.com/sites/warrenbobrow/2020/05/13/al-harrington-founder-of-viola-cannabis-digs-deeply-into-five-questions/?sh=342be3ff584b.

Draper, Kevin, and Juliet Macur. "Sha'Carri Richardson, a Track Sensation, Tests Positive for Marijuana." *New York Times*. July 1, 2021. https://www.nytimes.com/2021/07/01/sports/olympics/shacarri-richardson-suspended-marijuana.html.

Gaydos, Ryan. "Ex-NFL Star Ricky Williams on How Cannabis Use Changed His Mindset, Helped Him Deal with Anxiety." Fox News Sports, May 12, 2022. https://www.foxnews.com/sports/ricky-williams-cannabis-changed-mindset-deal-social-anxiety.

Hanna, Jason, and Anna Chernova. "Brittney Griner's Pretrial Detention in Russia Has Been Extended by a Month, Russian State News Reports." CNN Sports, May 13, 2022. https://edition.cnn.com/2022/05/13/sport/brittney-griner-russia-detention-extended/index.html.

Jaeger, Kyle. "NBA Won't Randomly Drug Test Players for Marijuana for Another Season, League Announces." Marijuana Moment, October 6, 2021. https://www.marijuanamoment.net/nba-wont-randomly-drug-test-players-for-marijuana-for-another-season-league-announces/.

———. "NFL Awards $1 Million to Study Marijuana Pain Management and Concussion Protection for Players." Marijuana Moment, February 1, 2022. https://www.marijuanamoment.net/nfl-awards-1-million-to-study-marijuana-pain-management-and-concussion-protection-for-players/.

McCann, Michael. "What's Next for Dion Waiters after Gummy Incident?" *Sports Illustrated*, November 11, 2019. https://www.si.com/nba/2019/11/11/dion-waiters-miami-heat-gummy-incident.

Pickman, Ben. "Al Harrington and the Fight for Cannabis Use in the NBA." *Sports Illustrated*, March 11, 2020. https://www.si.com/nba/2020/03/11 /al-harrington-cannabis-viola-adam-silver-nba.

Smith, Corbin. "Portland Sportswriters Once Shamed Black Athletes for Smoking Pot. What Do They Say Now?" *Portland (OR) Willamette Week*, January 17, 2018. https://www.wweek.com/sports/2018/01/17/portland-sportswriters -once-shamed-black-athletes-for-smoking-pot-what-do-they-say-now/.

Steinberg, Dan. "'All My Best Games I Was Medicated': Matt Barnes on His Game-Day Use of Marijuana." *Washington Post*, April 20, 2018. https://www .washingtonpost.com/news/early-lead/wp/2018/04/20/all-my-best-games -i-was-medicated-matt-barnes-on-his-game-day-use-of-marijuana/.

Stoudamire, Damon. "Letter to My Younger Self." Player's Tribune, March 16, 2016. https://www.theplayerstribune.com/articles/damon-stoudamire-nba -letter-to-my-younger-self.

Tracy, Jeff. "Where It Stands: Weed Policies by U.S. Sports League." Axios, October 20, 2021. https://www.axios.com/weed-policies-sports-leagues-nba -mlb-nfl-nhl-d4323e10-9b38-41ae-a35b-d3739c177dda.html.

Yakowicz, Will. "How Former NBA Star Al Harrington Is Building a $100 Million Team of Black Cannabis Entrepreneurs." *Forbes*, April 20, 2022. https://www.forbes.com/sites/willyakowicz/2022/04/20/nba-star-al -harrington-viola-100-black-cannabis-millionaires/?sh=754a48de451a.

Chapter 6: Nutritious and Delicious Eats
Joline Rivera

Chaey, Christina. "Everything You Need to Know about How to Eat Hemp Seeds." *Bon Appétit*, May 11, 2015. https://www.bonappetit.com/test-kitchen /ingredients/article/hemp-seeds.

Duvall, Chris. *Cannabis*. London: Reaktion Books, 2014.

Fine, Doug. *American Hemp Farmer: Adventures and Misadventures in the Cannabis Trade*. White River Junction, VT: Chelsea Green, 2020.

Graber, Cynthia, and Nicola Twilley. "Baked: How Pot Brownies and Pate de Fruits Fueled an Edible Cannabis Revolution." *Gastropod*, August 3, 2021. https://gastropod.com/baked-how-pot-brownies-and-pate-de-fruits-fueled -an-edible-cannabis-revolution/.

Lewis, Amanda Chicago. "A Hidden Origin Story of the CBD Craze." *New York Times*, May 23, 2020. https://www.nytimes.com/2020/05/23/sunday-review /coronavirus-cbd-oil.html.

Project CBD. Accessed May 16, 2022. https://www.projectcbd.org/.

Quarneti, Franca. "More Sustainability, Less Carbon: BMW Hemp and Recycling." Benzinga, July 27, 2022. Originally published in Spanish by El Planteo. https://www.benzinga.com/general/biotech/21/09/22832683 /more-sustainability-less-carbon-bmw-commits-to-hemp-and-recycling.

Rao, Ankita. "India's 'High' Holiday." *Atlantic*, March 17, 2014. https://www .theatlantic.com/international/archive/2014/03/indias-high-holiday/284448/.

Sanchez, Rudy. "Marijuana vs. Hemp: What's the Difference?" *Chicago Tribune*, August 15, 2019. https://www.chicagotribune.com/marijuana/sns-tft-whats-the -difference-marijuana-hemp-20190815-nljrmyx7hvdedhca4vhwqj4a3e-story.html.

Chapter 7: Material with Which You Can Build a House
Stephen Clarke

Brandon, Elissaveta M. "A New Building in France Makes the Case for Hemp to Replace Concrete." *Fast Company*, December 16, 2021. https://www .fastcompany.com/90706461/a-new-building-in-france-makes-the-case-for -hemp-to-replace-concrete.

Brownell, Blaine. "Hemp: The Next Disruptor in Construction after Wood?" *Architect*, October 28, 2021. https://www.architectmagazine.com/technology /hemp-the-next-disruptor-in-construction-after-wood_o.

Matloff, Judith. "Will Hempcrete Ever Catch On?" *Modern Farmer*, December 1, 2021. https://modernfarmer.com/2021/12/will-hempcrete-ever-catch-on/.

"Mexico High Court Clears Low-THC Cannabis Production." Hemp Industry Daily, December 6, 2021. https://hempindustrydaily.com/mexico-high-court -clears-low-thc-cannabis-production/.

Popescu, Adam. "There's No Place like Home, Especially If It's Made of Hemp." *New York Times*, January 29, 2018. https://www.nytimes.com/2018/01 /29/science/hemp-homes-cannabis.html.

Sparrow, Alex, and William Stanwix. *The Hempcrete Book: Designing and Building with Hemp-Lime*. Cambridge, UK: Green Books, 2014.

Chapter 8: Indigenous Empowerment
Mary Jane Oatman

Barcott, Bruce. "Inside Alderville, Canada's First Nations Cannabis Boomtown." Leafly, October 30, 2018. https://www.leafly.com/news/canada/inside-alderville -canadas-first-nations-cannabis-boomtown.

Bloom, Steve. "High Times Greats: John Trudell." *High Times*, February 12, 2021. https://hightimes.com/culture/john-trudell/.

Browne, Rachel. "Black and Indigenous People Are Overrepresented in Canada's Weed Arrests." *Vice*, April 18, 2018. https://www.vice.com/en/article/d35eyq/black-and-indigenous-people-are-overrepresented-in-canadas-weed-arrests.

Curtis, Christopher. "In Kanesatake, a Marijuana Dispensary Sprouts on Mohawk Land." *Montreal Gazette*, April 20, 2018. https://montrealgazette.com/news/local-news/marijuana-dispensary-on-mohawk-territory.

Donohue, Caitlin. "Decolonizing Cannabis." Breach, August 4, 2022. https://breachmedia.ca/decolonizing-cannabis/.

Fertig, Natalie. "Tribes Left Behind by America's Marijuana Laws." *Politico*, April 5, 2022. https://www.politico.com/news/2022/04/05/tribes-marijuana-laws-00022899.

Head, Bruce. "The 'Green Mile' Is the Cannabis Tourism Destination of the Kawarthas." kawarthaNOW, March 3, 2019. https://kawarthanow.com/2019/03/03/the-green-mile-alderville-first-nation/.

LaDuke, Winona. "The Renaissance of Tribal Hemp." *In These Times*, April 21, 2018. https://inthesetimes.com/article/industrial-hemp-native-american-tribes-winona-laduke.

Madden-Smith, Zoe. "Māori Company Granted New Zealand's First Medicinal Cannabis Licence." *Vice*, August 26, 2018. https://www.vice.com/en/article/mb4dn3/maori-company-granted-new-zealands-first-medicinal-cannabis-license.

"Map of All Indigenous Cannabis Dispensaries." Dispensing Freedom. Accessed August 30, 2022. https://dispensingfreedom.com/directory/.

Tribal Hemp and Cannabis Magazine. Nez Perce Reservation, Indigenous Cannabis Coalition, 2020–present.

Virdi, Jasmine. "Tracing the History of Marijuana in Mexico with Nidia Olvera Hernández." Chacruna Institute for Psychedelic Plant Medicines, April 9, 2021. https://chacruna.net/history_marijuana_mexico_pipiltzintzintli/.

Chapter 9: Fashion
Andrés Rivera

Associated Press. "Hemp and High Fashion Ruled the Runway." *Today*, February 1, 2008. https://www.today.com/news/hemp-high-fashion-ruled-runway-wbna22952534.

———."Sneaker Madness: Drug Chief Asks Adidas to Drop Hemp Name." *Los Angeles Times*, January 13, 1996. https://www.latimes.com/archives/la-xpm-1996-01-13-fi-24085-story.html.

Bump, Philip. "The Squares Lose: Hemp Flag to Grace Capitol Building on July 4th." *Atlantic*, July 2, 2013. https://www.theatlantic.com/national/archive/2013/07/hemp-flag-capitol-july-4/313711/.

Carreon, Mary. "Carbon Correction: The Cannabis and Climate Connection No One Is Talking About." *St. Louis Riverfront Times*, May 18, 2022. https://www.riverfronttimes.com/weed/carbon-correction-the-cannabis-and-climate-connection-no-one-is-talking-about-37732566.

Chun, Rene. "World's Oldest Fabric Is Now Its Newest." *New York Times*, June 25, 1995. https://www.nytimes.com/1995/06/25/archives/worlds-oldest-fabric-is-now-its-newest.html.

Drotleff, Laura. "Patagonia Is Working to Bring the Hemp Fiber Industry Back to the United States." MJ Biz Daily, July 1, 2021. https://mjbizdaily.com/patagonia-working-to-bring-hemp-fiber-to-united-states/.

"Hemp." *Encyclopaedia Britannica*, September 21, 2021. https://www.britannica.com/plant/hemp.

Khanna, Jasreen Mayal. "Can Hemp Be the Textile of the Future?" *Vogue India*, November 20, 2018. https://www.vogue.in/content/can-hemp-be-the-textile-of-the-future.

Ruscitto, Andriana. "Nike Unveils New Shoes Made from Hemp." *Cannabis Business Times*, March 23, 2022. https://www.cannabisbusinesstimes.com/article/nikes-latest-shoe-release-made-from-woven-hemp-fabric-airforce-1-blazer-mid/#:~:text=In%20August%202020%2C%20the%20company,and%20GOAT%20for%20over%20%24250.

Saragi, Dario. "Levi's Aims to Use More Hemp for Its Fashion Collections." *Forbes*, October 12, 2021. https://www.forbes.com/sites/dariosabaghi/2021/10/12/levis-jeans-company-aims-to-use-more-hemp-for-its-fashion-collections/?sh=6c6fa5a25756.

Chapter 10: Narco Ballads . . . and a Religious Icon
Ely Quintero

Beittel, June S. "Mexico: Organized Crime and Drug Trafficking Organizations." Congressional Research Service. Updated July 28, 2020. https://crsreports.congress.gov/product/pdf/R/R41576/45.

Borunda, Daniel. "Who Is Jesus Malverde? Question on Narco-Saint Hangs over 'Chapo' Guzman Drug Cartel Trial." *El Paso (TX) Times*, June 18, 2018. https://www.elpasotimes.com/story/news/crime/2018/06/18/chapo-guzman -trial-jury-asked-who-jesus-malverde-narcosaint-patron-saint-drug-dealers /703959002/.

CNN Editorial Research. "Mexico Drug War Fast Facts." CNN World. Last updated March 20, 2022. https://edition.cnn.com/2013/09/02/world/americas /mexico-drug-war-fast-facts/index.html.

Donohue, Caitlin. "Behind the Scenes of Ely Quintero's Corrido for CDMX Reggaetonera Rosa Pistola." *Remezcla*, April 24, 2020. https://remezcla.com /features/music/ely-quintero-rosa-pistola-corrido/.

———. "New DEA Report Says Border Seizures of Mexican Weed Have Fallen by 80 Percent." Merry Jane, March 5, 2021. https://merryjane.com/news/new -dea-report-says-border-seizures-of-mexican-weed-have-fallen-by-80-percent.

———. "This 420, We Need to Be Listening to Green Corridos." *High Times*, April 19, 2019. https://hightimes.com/culture/music/420-we-need-listening -green-corridos/.

Lakhani, Nina, and Erubiel Tirado. "Mexico's War on Drugs: What Has It Achieved and How Is the US Involved?" *Guardian* (US edition), December 8, 2016. https://www.theguardian.com/news/2016/dec/08/mexico-war-on-drugs -cost-achievements-us-billions.

Linares, Albinson. "Violent Crimes Rise in Mexico; 94.8% Go Unpunished." NBC News, October 11, 2021. https://www.nbcnews.com/news/latino/violent -crimes-rise-mexico-948-go-unpunished-rcna2846.

Murphy, Kate. "Mexican Robin Hood Figure Gains a Kind of Notoriety in U.S." *New York Times*, February 8, 2008. https://www.nytimes.com/2008/02 /08/us/08narcosaint.html.

Preiss, Danielle. "Shiva Is a God Who Likes Marijuana—And So Do Many of His Followers." *Goats and Soda*, National Public Radio, March 7, 2016. https:// www.npr.org/sections/goatsandsoda/2016/03/07/469519964/shiva-is-a-god -who-likes-marijuana-and-so-do-many-of-his-followers.

Valencia, Jorge. "In Mexico, the Unending Drug War Takes Its Toll with Thousands of Disappearances." *World*, July 21, 2020. https://theworld.org /stories/2020-07-21/mexico-unending-drug-war-takes-its-toll-thousands -disappearances.

Chapter 11: The Stories behind the Reggae Anthems
Firstman

Andres Henao, Luis, and Kwasi Gyamfi Asiedu. "Rastafari Want More Legal Marijuana for Freedom of Worship." *U.S. News & World Report*, December 10, 2021. https://www.usnews.com/news/us/articles/2021-12-10/rastafari-want -more-legal-marijuana-for-freedom-of-worship.

Associated Press. "Jamaica Decriminalises Marijuana." *Guardian* (US edition), February 5, 2015. https://www.theguardian.com/world/2015/feb/25/jamaica -decriminalises-marijuana.

Barrett, Leonard E. *The Rastafarians*. Boston: Beacon, 1977.

Chappell, Kate. "As Jamaica Looks to Cash In on Cannabis, Rastafarians Fear Being Left Out." Reuters, April 19, 2019. https://www.reuters.com/article/us -jamaica-cannabis-indigenous-idUSKCN1RW001.

Duvall, Chris S. *The African Roots of Marijuana*. Durham, NC: Duke University Press, 2019.

Elassar, Alaa. "Jamaica's High Court Ruled a School Was Legally Right in Banning a Child with Dreadlocks." CNN World, August 4, 2020. https://edition .cnn.com/2020/08/04/world/jamaica-dreadlocks-ban-student-trnd/index.html.

Fraser, Narissa. "Rastas Query Need for Licence to Use Ganja as Sacrament." *Trinidad and Tobago Newsday*, April 25, 2022. https://newsday.co.tt/2022/04/25 /rastas-query-need-for-licence-to-use-ganja-as-sacrament/.

McKeon, Lucy. "The True Story of Rastafari." *New York Review of Books*, January 6, 2017. https://www.nybooks.com/daily/2017/01/06/the-true-story -of-rastafari/?lp_txn_id=1323424.

Paley, Dawn Marie. "Canada's Cannabis Colonialism." *Toward Freedom*, October 8, 2019. https://towardfreedom.org/story/canadas-cannabis-colonialism/.

Chapter 12: The Reason Why You Went to Prison
Mauro Melgar

Braun, Martin Z., and Bloomberg. "Cannabis Taxes May Generate $12 Billion for U.S. States by 2030, According to Barclays Strategists." *Fortune*, December 3, 2021. https://fortune.com/2021/12/03/cannabis-taxes-generate-12-billion -by-2030-barclays-estimate/.

Corkery, Michael. "Oakland Cannabis Sellers, Once Full of Hope, Face a Harsh Reality." *New York Times*, March 15, 2022. https://www.nytimes.com /2022/03/15/business/cannabis-dispensaries-oakland.html.

Goode, Erich. "Pot and the Myth of Shen Nung." *New York Review of Books*, March 20, 2014. https://www.nybooks.com/articles/2014/03/20/pot-and-myth-shen-nung/.

Gramlich, John. "America's Incarceration Rate Falls to Lowest Level since 1995." Pew Research Center, August 16, 2021. https://www.pewresearch.org/fact-tank/2021/08/16/americas-incarceration-rate-lowest-since-1995/.

Kuhn, Casey. "The U.S. Spends Billions to Lock People Up, but Very Little to Help Them Once They're Released." *PBS NewsHour*, April 7, 2021. https://www.pbs.org/newshour/economy/the-u-s-spends-billions-to-lock-people-up-but-very-little-to-help-them-once-theyre-released.

Lekhtman, Alexander. "A Record Means Discrimination—But National Expungement Week Is Here." Filter, September 18, 2020. https://filtermag.org/national-expungement-week-2020/.

Lewis, Amanda Chicago. "Legalized Pot Was Supposed to Help Build Black Wealth in Los Angeles. It Failed." *New Republic*, April 4, 2022. https://newrepublic.com/article/165654/los-angeles-legal-marijuana-build-black-wealth-failed.

"Mauro Melgar Explains How National Expungement Week Helped Change His Life." *CashColorCannabis*, September 2019. https://open.spotify.com/episode/3zXKPAYrb23WL9LlAp5FF7.

McKinley, Jesse, and Grace Ashford. "New Yorkers with Marijuana Convictions Will Get First Retail Licenses." *New York Times*, March 9, 2022. https://www.nytimes.com/2022/03/09/nyregion/marijuana-sellers-licenses-hochul.html.

Minton, Todd D., Lauren G. Beatty, and Zhen Zeng. "Correctional Populations in the United States, 2019—Statistical Tables." US Department of Justice, July 2021. https://bjs.ojp.gov/sites/g/files/xyckuh236/files/media/document/cpus19st.pdf.

Morrison, Aaron. "50-Year War on Drugs Imprisoned Millions of Black Americans." Associated Press, July 23, 2021. https://apnews.com/article/war-on-drugs-75e61c224de3a394235df80de7d70b70.

"Rates of Drug Use and Sales, by Race; Rates of Drug Related Criminal Justice Measures, by Race." The Hamilton Project, Brookings Institution, October 21, 2016. https://www.hamiltonproject.org/charts/rates_of_drug_use_and_sales_by_race_rates_of_drug_related_criminal_justice.

Sigman, Zoe. "The Women Fighting for Cannabis Justice and Data Transparency in the U.S. Prison System." *Vogue*, April 20, 2021. https://www.vogue.com/article/cannabis-justice-data-transparency-us-prison-system.

Chapter 13: Protest
Miguel Fernández

Burns, Janet. "The Entrepreneur Who Brought Weed to Alaska Is Facing a 54-Year Sentence as Her Reward." *Forbes*, April 18, 2017. https://www.forbes.com/sites/janetwburns/2017/04/18/entrepreneur-who-brought-weed-industry-to-alaska-facing-54-year-sentence-as-her-reward/?sh=3f3f4b8953d7.

Campos, Isaac. *Home Grown: Marijuana and the Origins of Mexico's War on Drugs*. Chapel Hill: University of North Carolina Press, 2012.

Donohue, Caitlin. "Behind the 'M Word': The Forgotten Trans-Border History of Marijuana." *Remezcla*, April 20, 2018. https://remezcla.com/features/culture/behind-the-m-word-the-forgotten-trans-border-history-of-cannabis/.

———. "Inside Mexico's First Self-Proclaimed 'Cannabis Town.'" Merry Jane, December 17, 2021. https://merryjane.com/culture/inside-mexicos-first-self-declared-cannabis-town.

———. "Mexico City's First Weed Club to Use Courts to Spur Change." *High Times*, July 11, 2016. https://hightimes.com/culture/mexico-citys-first-weed-club-to-use-courts-to-spur-change/.

———. "Women Paved the Way for Mexico's Cannabis Legalization Movement, and Here's How They Did It." Merry Jane, April 13, 2021. https://merryjane.com/culture/women-paved-the-way-for-mexicos-cannabis-legalization-movement-and-heres-how-they-did-it.

Global Marijuana March. Facebook. Accessed May 3, 2022. https://www.facebook.com/GlobalMarihuanaMarch.

Laens, Ivonne Jeannot. "Pressure Mounts in Argentina's Courts and Streets to Legalize Cannabis for Personal Use." Global Press Journal, May 10, 2013. https://globalpressjournal.com/americas/argentina/pressure-mounts-in-argentina-s-courts-and-streets-to-legalize-cannabis-for-personal-use/.

Linthicum, Kate. "Mexico Is Poised to Become the Biggest Legal Marijuana Market in the World. Who Will Most Benefit?" *Los Angeles Times*, October 12, 2020. https://www.latimes.com/world-nation/story/2020-10-12/mexico-is-poised-to-become-the-biggest-legal-marijuana-market-in-the-world-the-big-question-who-will-benefit.

Robinson, Randy. "A Queer History of California's Medical Marijuana Movement." Merry Jane, May 2, 2019. https://merryjane.com/culture/a-queer-history-of-californias-medical-marijuana-movement.

Rodriguez Tardili, Santiago. "How Weed Activists Are Taking Action in the Mexican Legalization Movement." Leafly, March 26, 2021. https://www.leafly.com/news/politics/weed-activists-taking-action-in-mexican-cannabis-legalization.

Chapter 14: A Tool for Fighting Racism and Sexism
Luana Malheiro

Araujo, Felipe Neis. "Brazil Gains Ground on Medical Marijuana, in Defiance of Bolsonaro." Filter, July 6, 2021. https://filtermag.org/brazil-medical-marijuana-bolsonaro/.

Donohue, Caitlin. "Brazilian President Jair Bolsonaro's Regime Is Targeting Cannabis Activists and Users." Merry Jane, September 16, 2021. https://merryjane.com/news/brazilian-president-jair-bolsonaros-regime-is-targeting-cannabis-activists-and-users.

Franco, Anielle. "3 Years since Her Killing, the Legacy of Marielle Franco Is Black Women on the Frontline of Change." RioOnWatch, March 14, 2021. https://rioonwatch.org/?p=64861.

John, Tara, Rodrigo Pedroso, and Kareem El Damanhoury. "Brazilian President Luna Criticizes Police for Protesters' Breach of Government Buildings," CNN, January 10, 2023. https://edition.cnn.com/2023/01/10/americas/brazil-brasilia-police-congress-attack-intl-latam/index.html.

Lunardon, Jonas Araujo. "Maconha, Capoeira e Samba: a construção do proibicionismo como uma política de criminalização social" ["Marijuana, Capoeira and Samba: The Construction of Prohibitionism as a Policy of Social Criminalization"]. 1st International Seminary of Political Science, Federal University of Rio Grande do Sul, September 2015. https://www.ufrgs.br/sicp/wp-content/uploads/2015/09/LUNARDON-J.-Maconha-Capoeira-e-Samba-a-constru%C3%A7%C3%A3o-do-proibicionismo-como-uma-pol%C3%ADtica-de-criminaliza%C3%A7%C3%A3o-social.pdf.

Malheiro, Luana. *Tornar-se mulher usuária de crack: cultura e política sobre drogas*. Rio de Janeiro: Telha, 2020.

Muñoz, César. "From Rio, a Cautionary Tale on Police Violence." Human Rights Watch, August 15, 2021. https://www.hrw.org/news/2021/08/15/rio-cautionary-tale-police-violence.

Nugent, Ciara, and Thaís Regina. "How Black Brazilians Are Looking to a Slavery-Era Form of Resistance to Fight Racial Injustice Today." *Time*, December 16, 2020. https://time.com/5915902/brazil-racism-quilombos/.

Pauluze, Thaiza. "In Three Years, Police Killed at Least 2,215 Children and Adolescents in the Country." *Folha de Sao Paolo*, Grupo Folha, December 15, 2020. https://www1.folha.uol.com.br/internacional/en/brazil/2020/12 /in-three-years-police-killed-at-least-2215-children-and-adolescents-in -the-country.shtml.

Peet, Charlotte. "'Carnage': 25 Killed in Rio de Janeiro's Deadliest Police Raid." Al Jazeera, May 6, 2021. https://www.aljazeera.com/news/2021/5/6 /at-least-25-killed-in-rio-de-janeiros-deadliest-police-raid.

Putti, Alexandre. "Não se resolve o crack com política criminal e sim com acolhimento, diz antropóloga." *CartaCapital*, September 16, 2020. https://www .cartacapital.com.br/sociedade/nao-se-resolve-o-crack-com-politica-criminal -e-sim-com-acolhimento-diz-antropologa.

Rocha, Lia De Mattos. "The Life and Battles of Marielle Franco." openDemocracy, March 20, 2019. https://www.opendemocracy.net/en /democraciaabierta/life-and-battles-marielle-franco/.

Tsavkko Garcia, Raphael. "New Wave of Far-Right Attacks on Cannabis in Brazil Threaten Medical Use." *Cannabis Health*, August 23, 2021. https:// cannabishealth.com/new-far-right-attacks-cannabis-in-brazil/.

Chapter 15: A Way to Learn about Global Politics
Froylán Rascón

Bieschke, Marke. *Into the Streets: A Young Person's Visual History of Protest in the United States.* Minneapolis: Zest Books, 2020.

Contreras, Geras, and Theo Di Castri, hosts. "Expanding Harm-Reduction Education and Youth Participation." In *Behind the Pages*, April 20, 2021. https:// soundcloud.com/user-393825985/expandin-harm-reduction-education-and -youth-participation.

Di Castri, Theo. "Catalyst: Expanding Harm-Reduction Education and Youth Participation in the Context of the War on Drugs." *Journal on Education in Emergencies* 6, no. 1 (October 2020). http://hdl.handle.net/2451/61510.

"Forced Displacement in Colombia More Than Doubled in 2021: Report." Al Jazeera, February 16, 2022. https://www.aljazeera.com/news/2022/2/16/forced -displacement-in-colombia-more-than-doubled-in-2021-report.

Rodríguez Gómez, Diana, and Theo di Castri. "Youth Voices: Rethinking the War on Drugs. A Catalyst Curriculum Guide." Institute of Latin American Studies, Columbia University, July 26, 2021. https://academiccommons .columbia.edu/doi/10.7916/d8-jww9-5r77.

Sawyer, Wendy, and Peter Wagner. "Mass Incarceration: The Whole Pie 2022." Prison Policy Initiative, March 14, 2022. https://www.prisonpolicy.org /reports/pie2022.html.

"Timeline: America's War on Drugs." National Public Broadcasting, April 2, 2007. https://www.npr.org/templates/story/story.php?storyId=9252490.

Chapter 16: How Moms Change the World
Ana Álvarez

Bienenstock, David. "5 Cannabis Moms Who Changed the Game." Leafly, May 10, 2019. https://www.leafly.com/news/lifestyle/cannabis-moms-who -changed-the-game.

Fox, Hayley. "Weed and Pregnancy: How Cannabis Laws Are Hurting Mothers." *Rolling Stone*, November 17, 2018. https://www.rollingstone.com/culture /culture-features/weed-pregnancy-mother-family-marijuana-cannabis-755697/.

Hasse, Javier. "Meet the Brave Moms Leading the Fight for Cannabis Legislation in Latin America." *Forbes*, April 9, 2020. https://www.forbes.com /sites/javierhasse/2020/04/09/mama-cultiva/?sh=68889bad4ba6.

Kelleher, Olivia. "Vera Twomey Celebrates after Dutch Medicinal Cannabis Funded Up Front." *Irish Times*, July 20, 2021. https://www.irishtimes.com /news/health/vera-twomey-celebrates-after-dutch-medicinal-cannabis-funded -up-front-1.4625574.

Norton, Amy. "Why Are More Women Using Pot, Other Cannabis Products during Pregnancy?" *U.S. News & World Report*, December 20, 2021. https:// www.usnews.com/news/health-news/articles/2021-12-20/why-are-more -women-using-pot-other-cannabis-products-during-pregnancy.

Partlow, Joshua. "An 8-Year-Old's Tragic Illness Tests Mexico's Ban on Marijuana Use." *Washington Post*, August 28, 2015. https://www.washingtonpost .com/world/the_americas/an-8-year-olds-tragic-illness-tests-mexicos-ban-on -marijuana-use/2015/08/28/af6b705a-411f-11e5-9f53-d1e3ddfd0cda_story.html.

Schwenk, Katja. "Mother Accused of Child Neglect for Pot Use while Pregnant Wins Appeal." *Phoenix New Times*, April 1, 2022. https://www .phoenixnewtimes.com/marijuana/phoenix-woman-accused-of-child-neglect -for-medical-marijuana-use-wins-appeal-13343938.

Weinberg, Bill. "A Mother's Courage in Peru: Facing Prison for Giving Her Son Medical Marijuana." *High Times*, August 23, 2018. https://hightimes.com/activism /mothers-courage-peru-facing-prison-giving-her-son-medical-marijuana/.

Chapter 17: Groundbreaking Politics
Diego Olivera

Bonello, Deborah. "Weed-Curious Politicians Should Look to Uruguay, Where There's No Fuss over Legal Pot." *Vice*, November 5, 2019. https://www.vice.com/en/article/ywa4yg/weed-curious-politicians-should-look-to-uruguay-where-theres-no-fuss-over-legal-pot.

Laqueur, Hannah, Ariadne Rivera-Aguirre, Aaron Sheva, Alvaro Castillo-Carniglia, Kara E. Rudolph, Jessica Ramirez, Silvia S. Martins, and Magdalena Cerdá. "The Impact of Cannabis Legalization in Uruguay on Adolescent Cannabis Use." *International Journal of Drug Policy* 80 (June 2020). https://www.sciencedirect.com/science/article/abs/pii/S095539592030089X.

Maybin, Simon. "Uruguay: The World's Marijuana Pioneer." BBC News, April 4, 2019. https://www.bbc.com/news/business-47785648.

Olivera, Diego. "Opinión: A tres años del comienzo de la venta de marihuana en farmacias." Montevideo Portal, July 20, 2020. https://www.montevideo.com.uy/Columnistas/Opinion--A-tres-anos-del-comienzo-de-la-venta-de-marihuana-en-farmacias-uc759027.

Parks, Ken. "Uruguay Wants to Open Pot Market to Tourists: Cannabis Weekly." Bloomberg, September 13, 2021. https://www.bloomberg.com/news/articles/2021-09-13/uruguay-wants-to-open-pot-market-to-tourists-cannabis-weekly.

Pascual, Alfredo. "Three Years in, Uruguay's Recreational Cannabis Market 'Tangible' Success." MJ Biz Daily. Updated December 17, 2021. https://mjbizdaily.com/3-years-after-legalization-uruguays-recreational-cannabis-market-tangible-success/.

von Hoffmann, Jonas. "'Someone Has to Be the First': Tracing Uruguay's Marijuana Legalisation through Counterfactuals." *Journal of Politics in Latin America* 12, no. 2 (October 7, 2020). https://journals.sagepub.com/doi/full/10.1177/1866802X20937415.

Additional Resources

If you're looking for more information on cannabis justice, health information related to weed, or what's happening with the drug in the political world, these organizations from around the American continents can help. Some of the organizations with which this book's interviewees are involved or mentioned in our talks are also on this list.

Americans for Safe Access
https://www.safeaccessnow.org

Athletes for CARE
https://athletesforcare.org

Bay Area Latino Cannabis Alliance
https://balca.live

Buscando Esperanza on Facebook
https://www.facebook.com/people/Buscando-Esperanza
-Per%C3%BA/100064770606211/

Cage-Free Cannabis
https://www.cagefreecannabis.com

Cannabis Workers Coalition
https://www.cannabisworkerscoalition.org

Cannaclusive
https://www.cannaclusive.com

Cannativa
https://cannativa.net

Catalyst
https://www.catalyst-catalizador.org

Dispensing Freedom
https://dispensingfreedom.com

Drug Policy Alliance
https://drugpolicy.org

Échele Cabeza
https://echelecabeza.com

Heavengrown Hemp Architecture
http://heavengrown.com

Last Prisoner Project
https://www.lastprisonerproject.org

Mamá Cultiva Argentina
https://www.mamacultivaargentina.org

Marijuana Moment
https://www.marijuanamoment.net

Marijuana Policy Project
https://www.mpp.org

National Expungement Works
https://newxnow.org

National Institutes of Health
https://nida.nih.gov/research-topics/cannabis-marijuana

Plantón 420
https://www.planton420.org

Rastafari Indigenous Village
https://rastavillage.com

Rede Nacional de Feministas Antiproibicionistas
https://renfa.org

Regulación por la Paz
http://regulacionporlapaz.com

ReverdeSer Colectivo
http://reverdeser.org

The Social Impact Center
https://www.thesocialimpactcenter.org

Students for Sensible Drug Policy
https://ssdp.org

Supernova Women
https://www.supernovawomen.com

Todos Hacemos Cultura
https://todoshacemoscultura.com

Women Grow
https://womengrow.com

Index

Photo Acknowledgments

Image credits: Edwin Remsberg/Getty Images, p. 11; Boris Roessler/picture alliance/Getty Images, p. 12; Gainew Gallery/Alamy Stock Photo, p. 19; Courtesy of D'Arcy Hamilton, p. 20; Courtesy of Clara Gomila, p. 30; Niall Carson/PA Images/Getty Images, p. 31; Sara Stathas/Alamy Stock Photo, p. 36; Alberto Vargas, p. 38; Michael Macor/The San Francisco Chronicle/ Getty Images, p. 44; Nico Malazartes, p. 46; David Paul Morris/Bloomberg/ Getty Images, p. 51; Patrick Smith/Getty Images, p. 57; Frank Lawlor, p. 61; Akvals/Shutterstock, p. 63; Photo by Matt Armendariz; Food Styling by Adam Pearson, p. 64; Photo by Eva Kolenko; Food styling by Adam Pearson, p. 65; Jessica Loijens/iStock/Getty Images, p. 69; Wirestock, Inc./Alamy Stock Photo, p. 70; Mark Rightmire/MediaNews Group/Orange County Register/Getty Images, p. 77; Courtesy of Todos Hacemos Cultura, p. 85; Photo by Rob Loud/Getty Images, p. 90; RASHIDE FRIAS/AFP/Getty Images, p. 94; Photo by Ernesto Olivares. Editing by María Fernanda Molins, p. 95; Charlie Steiner - Hwy 67 Revisited/Getty Images, p. 102; Courtesy of Rastafari Indigenous, p. 104; ALFREDO ESTRELLA/AFP/Getty Images, p. 119; Courtesy of Plantón 420, p. 120; Lazyllama/Alamy Stock Photo, p. 129; Courtesy of RENFA, p. 131; Fabio Vieira/FotoRua/NurPhoto/Getty Images, p. 135; Courtesy of Catalyst, p. 138; Courtesy of Buscando Esperanza, p. 145; Courtesy of P., p. 152; Mashikomo/Shutterstock, p. 169.

Cover: Yarygin/Shutterstock.

About the Author

Caitlin Donohue is a bilingual culture journalist whose recent work focuses on drug politics and education. Her weekly Spanish language radio show *Crónica* examines psychoactive substances in times of prohibition and airs on Radio Nopal, one of Mexico's largest independent web stations. She started working as a union organizer as a teenager. In her twenties, she began her journalism career as an intern at the *San Francisco Bay Guardian* alternative weekly newspaper, where she eventually became culture editor. It was there that Donohue started writing about weed for her column "Herbwise"—kicking off a journey that, years later, would bring her to become a two-time judge for the Mexican Cannabis Cup.

She has contributed to publications including *High Times, Remezcla, Rookie, Advocate, Marie Claire, FACT,* and the McSweeney's anthology *Indelible in the Hippocampus: Writings from the Me Too Movement.* Donohue believes that culture writing has the power to reframe reality. Her first book for young adults was *She Represents: 43 Women Who Are Changing Politics . . . and the World,* a collection of biographies of women who lead governments. She was raised in the San Francisco Bay Area, has lived on four continents, and has made a home in Mexico City with her cat, Kiara, since 2014.